ALFA ROMEO
SPIDER

Other Titles in the Crowood AutoClassics Series

ALFA ROMEO
Spider
The Complete Story

John Tipler

First published in 1998 by
The Crowood Press Ltd
Ramsbury, Marlborough
Wiltshire SN8 2HR

British Library Cataloguing-in-Publication Data
A catalogue record for this book is available from the British
Library.

ISBN 1 86126 1225

Typeface used: New Century Schoolbook

Typeset and designed by
Harvey de Roemer at JP3 Ltd
Chelsea Reach
79-89 Lots Road
London SW10 0RN

Printed and bound by The Bath Press

Contents

Acknowledgements

How can one not have fun doing a book about Spiders? It was all most enjoyable, and undoubtedly one of life's quality tasks, and I'd like to thank everyone who contributed to it. In no particular order, my appreciation goes to Michael Lindsay of the Alfa Romeo Owners' Club for liaison and for delving deep into his Spider files for some of those all-important previously unpublished photos; Jon Day at the National Motor Museum, Beaulieu, for providing archive and current photographs of the cars; Huguette Boyagis and her colleagues at Alfa Romeo GB for archive photographs and loan of a current Spider press car; Fiat Corporate Communications Director Richard Gadeselli for production statistics; Francesco Pagni of Pininfarina's PR department for some high-quality transparencies and archive shots; David Sparrow for the transparencies taken during our test session at Lydden Hill circuit and the Kent countryside; Nathan Morgan for snapping the Earl's Court pictures; Dawn Stanley for her Spider photography at Blickling Hall, Holkham and Blakeney; Chris Pickett for the 4R Zagato pic and US-spec concours winner at Stanford Hall; Mike Spenceley and Jeff Sheridan of MGS Coachworks for a raft of restoration pictures (which ones to choose?) and counselling on current methodology; Alan Bennett of Benalfa Cars, David Edgington of EB Spares (The Italian Connection), Chris Sweetapple and John Timpany for restoration anecdotes; Bobby Bell of importers Bell and Colvill on historical background and the left-hand-drive connection; Dermot Golden for tales of the Wild West and the use of his California Spiders; and lastly, Andy Cameron and Helen for their generous hospitality after a photo-session at Lydden Hill circuit, Kent. Finally, this one is dedicated to my wife Laura.

Introduction

On a sunny day there's little to match the thrill of meandering down country lanes or blatting along fast open roads in a sports car. And if that sports car is an Alfa Spider, so much the better. No one can match Alfa Romeo when it comes to building sports cars, and there are few things as quintessentially Italianate as the Spider. Alfa Romeo have been at it consistently since the advent of the Giulietta in 1955, and with the latest incarnation launched on the growing wave of soft-top popularity in 1994, the concept has been brought bang up to date.

Alfa Spiders have always been drivers' cars. Traditionally, there was always good access to the cockpit. Where some sports cars could be defined as cramped and old-fashioned, accessibility to the Spider has always been good. Its top came down with no problems, you had an adequate driving position – which some would define as typically Italianate – and the rasping twin-cam engine started easily and provided a delightful sound track. And changing gear with the 105-series gearshift is still, some

A tale of two Spiders is about to unfold, as Mr and Mrs Tipler prepare for an outing, courtesy of Bell and Colvill – but in which car?

The distinctive Pininfarina styling made the new Spider one of the most striking machines on the road during the late 1990s. Viewed in profile, it looks as though the engine could have been located amidships, like the Elise or MGF.

thirty years on, at least as pleasant a shift as you'll find on any classic car.

It's hard to pinpoint the heyday of the old Spider. Perhaps it was 1969, when it was in its most elegant round-tail 1750 form, although more units were produced in the 1980s and for that reason, this car may be the archetype. It may not feel like a modern car now, especially alongside the contemporary Spider, but in its day its looks and specification placed it some way ahead of the field. Today, the classic models can still provide thrills, but in a different way from modern sports cars, and it can still fight its corner against many of them.

The size and proportions of the old Spiders always seemed correct for a roadster. An E-type was over-long and over-flash, dubbed a penis-extension in some quarters, while the Austin Healey 3000 and the Triumph TR6 were macho muscle-builders. The Elan was every bit a driver's car, but it was too cramped inside and of questionable reliability. An MGB or TR4 might have been acceptable size-wise, but they weren't anything like as sophisticated as the Alfa. The performance of both the Pininfarina-styled Fiat 124 Spider and the Jensen-Healey was comparable, but neither could match the Alfa's flair. And for all its 'hand-built by craftsmen' qualities, the Morgan's appearance was just a bit too old-fashioned for many people. Besides, there was always that waiting list before you could get your hands on a new one. In some ways, you might buy a classic Alfa Spider today for the same reasons as you would buy a Morgan: you'd be getting hand-built, open-air motoring of a particular period feel and experience.

There were other soft-top sports cars available in the mid-sixties as well, including the Triumph Spitfire, Datsun 1600, Sunbeam Alpine and the Lotus Super Seven. The classic Spider's real sibling was the Fiat 124 Spider, built literally alongside

in the Pininfarina factory, and sold mainly
in the United States, but never imported
into Britain. It is not possible to make the
same statement about Fiat's latest Spider –
the Barchetta – and the new Alfa model,
however. The Fiat is smaller this time, and
its stylistic hallmarks are perhaps closer to
those of the BMW Z3, more retrospective
than forward-looking. However, the current
Fiat Coupé and new Alfa GTV do have a
little more in common stylistically. The new
Alfa Spider is possibly closer in this respect
to the second-generation Elan, or perhaps
the more expensive Porsche Boxter would
do as a comparison. Even so, the Porsche
model manages to be both advanced in
concept as well as harking back to the RSK
racing models of the late 1950s. And,
needless to say, it is in a different price
league to the Arese-built car.

Unlike most Porsches, the Alfa Spider has
little in the way of a competition history.
This is due as much to its character as a
hedonistic pleasure vehicle as to the fact
that the factory produced cars eminently
more suitable for Touring Car and Sports
Prototype racing in the GTA, TI Super, and
the Tipo 33-series. However, a few have
cropped up over the years, notably in the
USA, and I have tried to set them in the
context of the Spider's history.

If the classic Alfa Spider had one disad-
vantage when it was in current production,
it was price, for they were always substan-
tially more expensive than their homegrown
contemporaries. You had to really want one
to go that bit extra for a Spider, otherwise
you would opt for one of those other symbols
of the 'swinging sixties', an E-Type or an
Elan. In the US in particular, its chief rival
during the late sixties and seventies was its
stablemate, the Fiat 124 Spider.

Towards the end of the life of the classic
Spider, a new breed of open-top rival
emerged with the renaissance of open-top

The Alfa Romeo Spider was in production for such a long time that it spanned several styling changes and increases in engine capacity and attained classic status on the way. Any of its different guises would provide a particular driving experience. Pictured are a 1987 Spider 2.0, a 1976 2000 model and a 1967 Duetto.

The new Spider – resplendent and centre-stage at the 1997 Earl's Court Motor Show.

sports cars in the early 1990s. Serious competition now came from the Mazda MX5 (Miata), the TVR S, and the second-generation Elan. As you would expect, all three were very competent in their own way, particularly the swift Elan. Some people would have added the Reliant Scimitar SST to this list, but, although quick, it was just too small for anyone who could remotely be described as tall. But although the quality was there in the MX5, and the marque history was present in the TVR and Lotus, somehow they lacked the pedigree, the ambience and the class of the Alfa Romeo. This was something which probably only the Morgan could equally lay claim to at the time.

Nowadays, if it's a modern, state-of-the-art drive you're after, you need look no further than the latest Alfa Spider. It might have just as many classy rivals as its predecessors did, in the shape of cars such as the BMW Z3, MGF or Lotus Elise, but the Alfa has the measure of them for looks and performance.

SPIDER OR SPYDER?

Perhaps it's as well to get one thing straight to start off with. We often see cars advertised in the 'for sale' columns as Alfa 'Spyders', and I think to myself that either the cars' owners or the magazines' classified staff ought to get it sorted out. (But when you come across 'Alpha' Romeo, you know for sure that they're beyond hope!) I have always regarded 'Spyder' as incorrect, and since the manufacturer calls them 'Spiders', this surely has to be the correct spelling. The term 'spider' is generic, and applies in Italy to a roadster, a car with a retractable or removable soft-top. The common usage of the spelling 'spyder' is considered inaccurate by many of the cognoscenti,

and in fact refers only to cars that Alfa Romeo exported to Germany. So that helps to explain why open-top Porsches are always Spyders, and not Spiders.

HALCYON DAYS

I have served my time as an Alfa owner, to this day, in Giulia and 75 saloons and GTV coupés of one sort or another, but my rag-roof motoring as a twenty-something was at the wheel of an Elan S4SE, various MGBs and an MGC. In the days when the Spider was young and so was I, I always seemed to be rushing around from pub to race track or wherever with a car full of people. I now reflect that this was the price one pays for owning a saloon car. However, I was more recently in a position to catch up on classic Spidering, thanks to a friend who garaged a number of Californian imports at my place, with carte blanche to cruise the country lanes on sunny days. It happened to coincide conveniently with researching this book, thus helping greatly with objective appraisals of the model in general, and, as we shall see, it provided an insight into the pitfalls of importing these allegedly rust-free 'dry-state' cars.

The Alfa Spider was always an interesting car, and destined for classic status by any criteria. It became such an icon that it was even possible to feel a touch daunted by the prospect of writing about it. Spider buffs tend to be connoisseurs who would quickly recognise factual errors, and, after all, what hadn't already been said? The scope of this book altered significantly shortly after commissioning when it became clear that neither Alfa Romeo nor Pininfarina were about to throw open the factory gates for me to view the production process. This is something I have been fortunate enough to be able to do with several of my other books, including Morgan, TVR, and Triumph Motorcycles. I believe it was a missed opportunity for some decent PR, if you'll excuse the sour grapes. Fiat's Corporate Communications boss Richard Gadeselli told me they had so many requests worldwide for access to the factory that the policy nowadays is no visits whatsoever. Not even a bona fide author? Sorry, no! What you have here then is, by default, a history of Spiders, incorporating a good many anecdotes and previously unpublished information, such as the low-down on the new generation of Spiders.

The classic Spider was unique, in that it not only remained in production virtually unchanged for a quarter of a century, but it managed to transcend that peculiar period in its life during the late-seventies and early-eighties when it was regarded as being somewhat passé and unfashionable. Rather like a butterfly from its chrysalis, it emerged gloriously from this era, soaring high on a wave of sixties nostalgia and an intense interest in anything remotely 'classic' during the late 1980s. It certainly set the stage for the arrival of Alfa's current model, which, along with its GTV stablemate, is undoubtedly one of the most striking cars on the roads in the late nineties.

The new Alfa Spider and its GTV stablemate were arguably the most striking sports cars on the road – or in this case, the beach – in the late 1990s.

Although clearly developed as two distinct models, the current GTV and Spider are mechanically the same, sharing Alfa's latest 1,970cc TwinSpark engine, which has two spark plugs and four valves per cylinder, variable valve timing, hydraulic tappets and the latest Bosch Motronic engine management system. Aside from competition use in the GTA, the modern twin-spark unit was honed in the 75, 164 and 155 saloons, and powered a fair number of Formula 3 single-seaters in the early 1990s. By 1996 it was being shoehorned into the new generation of Alfa compacts, the 145 and 146 models, in 1.6-, 1.8-, and 2.0-litre

capacity, while the standard-bearing 156 saloon – sadly not reviving the hallowed Giulietta name – also employs the latest iron-block version in 1.8- and 2.0-litre format.

Power output of the standard 2.0-litre engine is 150bhp at 6,200rpm, an improvement on the old twin-cam's relatively modest 130bhp, and giving the Spider a top speed of 130mph (210kph) and a 0-60mph (0-100kph) time of 8.4 seconds. However, one of the chief advantages of the new engine is that 90% of its torque is available at a low 2,500rpm, with maximum torque arriving at a relaxed 4,000rpm.

As befits all-new models in the increasingly high-tech and safety-conscious 1990s, both models feature driver and passenger airbags as original equipment, and the steering column is adjustable for both height and reach. Anyone familiar with traditional Alfas will have spent ages striving for that elusive compromise between steering wheel reach, pedals, gear lever and seat. Happily, this appears not to be a problem any more. Even the pedals are nicely spaced now.

The Spider chassis has also been endowed with an entirely new multi-link rear suspension system, while anti-lock brakes are standard. But as a sop to classic buffs, there is a touch of retro-styling about the hooded instrument clusters, angled towards the driver, with a nicely but none too radically designed flow about the dashboard and console ergonomics.

The Spider's excellent soft-top folds away inside the bodywork, in such a way that the car's dramatic styling is not compromised, although this is to a small degree at the expense of luggage space. The latter amounts to just 3.8 cubic feet (1.07 cubic metres), or in other words, a couple of overnight bags and a frisbee, but if you really wanted to carry more than the bare essentials for two, you'd have bought a 156, or just possibly a Ulysse MPV to accommodate the extended family.

Evolution

1955–1962	Alfa Romeo Giulietta Spider
	Veloce introduced 1956
1962–1965	Alfa Romeo Giulia Spider
1966–1967	Alfa Romeo Duetto
1967–1971	Alfa Romeo 1750 Spider Veloce
	Kamm-tail bodies introduced 1970
1974–1986	Alfa Romeo 1600 Spider
1968–1972 & 1977–1978	Alfa Romeo Spider 1300 Junior
1971–1993	Alfa Romeo 2000 Spider Veloce and Spider 2.0
1994 to date	Alfa Romeo Spider 2.0-litreTwinSpark 16V and 3.0-litre V6

1 A History of Alfa Romeo

This is something of a thumbnail sketch of the Alfa Romeo Spiders' long and distinguished ancestry, but helpful in tracing the lineage of the sports cars within the company's production history. Alfa Romeo joined Lancia and Fiat as one of Italy's top three volume car producers in 1950. This position was achieved when the firm moved into the modern world of production-line unit-construction with the 1900 Berlinas, followed soon afterwards in 1954 by the Giulietta models.

In 1987 the company was acquired by Fiat, after a takeover battle with Ford, from the Italian state-owned Finmeccanica group. Alfa was to join Lancia and Ferrari under the protective Fiat umbrella. But although Alfa Romeo's charismatic and often idiosyncratic

saloons have always earned the company's bread and butter, from the early 1950s at any rate, Alfa Romeo's reputation was founded on great feats on the world's race circuits and gruelling endurance events like the Mille Miglia and Targa Florio. Since then, its ongoing philosophy has been to build a range of sports and grand touring cars, which could be marketed alongside the saloons.

Alfa Romeo is Italy's third oldest sporting manufacturer, preceded only by Fiat and Itala. It was founded in 1910 as Anonima Lombarda Fabrica Automobili, providing the makings of that immortal acronym, ALFA. The company was originally set up in Naples as a subsidiary of the French Darracq concern in 1906, to sell off surplus cars, but the following year the operation

Lowering the engine and gearbox into a 101-series Giulia Sprint on the production line at Portello, 1963.

Introduced in 1987, the Alfa 75 was powered by 1.8- and 2.0-litre TwinSpark engines, as well as the 3.0-litre V6 like this Veloce version with the factory-fitted race-replica bodykit.

transferred to the labour-rich Milanese suburb of Portello. Insufficient demand for these fragile, underpowered French cars broke the fledgling company, and it was re-formed as ALFA by Ugo Stella, with Giuseppe Merosi as chief designer.

The first ALFAs were quite different from the pretty Darracqs; they were large and robust, with powerful engines and decent brakes, more appropriate for the poor state of the majority of Italian roads at the time. Merosi's first two cars were the 4.1-litre 24hp and the 2.4-litre 15hp models. Internally, these engines were not so far removed from the layout to which Alfa Romeo has remained faithful throughout its history:

twin overhead camshafts operating two rows of inclined valves, with hemispherical combustion chambers. ALFA's emblems even then were made up of the familiar red cross of St George, which was the arms of the city of Milan, combined with the medieval shield adornment of the Visconti family, which is a serpent devouring a child. The four-leaf clover or quadrifoglio motif that has always featured on Alfa Romeo competition cars appeared on engine and chassis numberplates.

In 1911, ALFA took its first step into the competition fray, entering two 24hp cars in the arduous Sicilian road race, the Targa Florio, and although one car led the race, both eventually retired. ALFA's first taste of competition success came in 1913 when Campari and Franchini came third and fourth in the Coppa Florio. If the advent of the First World War prevented Merosi's promising four-cylinder twin-cam Grand Prix car being raced, it also had the beneficial effect of introducing prosperous Milanese mining engineer Nicola Romeo to ALFA. By arrangement, Ing. Romeo took over the ALFA plant in 1915 to produce compressors, tractors and Isotta aircraft engines for the war effort. When the war was over, Nicola Romeo became managing director, and the company was from then onwards called Alfa Romeo.

ENTER ENZO

Two of the pre-war cars were entered for the 1919 Targa Florio, running without success, but things improved from the early 1920s, when the works Alfa Romeo team was run by one of its drivers, Enzo Ferrari. Race victories began with Campari's wins at Mugello in 1920 and 1921, and Sivocci won the Targa Florio the following year driving Merosi's new 3.0-litre six-cylinder type-RL. In 1924, Vittorio Jano's first design, the 2.0-litre supercharged straight-eight P2 won first time out at Cremona with Antonio Ascari at the wheel, and its first Grand Prix at Lyons driven by Campari. Although Ascari was killed in his P2 the following year at Montlhéry, the Alfa team had won sufficient races to gain the first ever World Championship. A fine achievement, although in those days racing was a more relaxed and broader-based affair than the tight-knit enclave it has more recently become. The company was justifiably proud, and marked their success with the addition of a laurel wreath to the Alfa Romeo badge. Curiously, few other firms

Alfa 155s being assembled on the robotized production line at Arese. Spiders and GTVs are also finished here.

have celebrated their competition successes to the same extent, even though race and rally victories undoubtedly sell cars. Admittedly, Jaguar has at times based its advertising on Le Mans wins, and Lotus certainly marked its World Championship wins on its road-going cars during the sixties and seventies, while Lancia to an extent capitalized on its World Rally successes.

JANO'S ALFAS

Whereas Merosi's road cars of the early 1920s were conceptually much the same as his pre-war cars – robust, heavy, and hardly sports cars – those of his successor Jano were different altogether, and much more closely related to the racing cars. The engines were shorn of their superchargers

If ever a design stood the test of time, it was the Duetto. The purity of line was never bettered, and the harmony of the 'boat-tail' echoing the rounded nose remains a stylistic masterpiece.

and two of their cylinders, and at first given only a set of vertical valves and a single camshaft, and endowed with open-top light-weight bodies on race-developed chassis. These were the 6C 1500 and 6C 1750 which appeared in 1927, soon to be superseded by twin-cam Super Sport and 100mph (160kph) Gran Sport versions. One of the most interesting of the pre-war Alfas was the 6C 1750 Gran Sport introduced in 1930, a convertible with aluminium bodywork by Zagato (among others), which possibly contributed most to the aura of racing that the company generated in the 1930s. This was the car with which Tazio Nuvolari dominated the 1930 Mille Miglia, heading three other works 1750 Gran Sports over the finishing line. In response to popular demand, Alfa built 159 limited edition supercharged derivatives, known as the 1750 Gran Turismo Compressore model, in 1931 and 1932, mostly with factory-made steel bodies. Among them was a saloon-bodied version, which was Alfa Romeo's, and arguably the world's, first grand touring car. Typically, the 1750 Gran Turismo was also the subject of styling exercises by major coachbuilders, including Touring-of-Milan, whose Spider version won first prize at the Villa d'Este Concours d'Elégance competition in 1931.

The works' competition programme was controlled by Enzo Ferrari, who had set up his racing headquarters at Modena in 1929 to run the factory Alfas and maintain customers' racing cars. It was an era in which Alfa Romeo virtually dominated international competition. The car which accomplished so much was Jano's 2.3-litre straight-eight 8C 2300, winning Le Mans in four consecutive years from 1931 to 1935. The Grand Prix version of the 8C won its first race, the 1931 European Grand Prix at Monza, and it was known as the Monza from then onwards. What was remarkable about the design of this engine was that it was basically made up of two four-cylinder twin-cam engines facing each other with the camshaft drive in the centre. The advantage of this curious layout was that it allowed for shorter cams and cranks, and was therefore in theory more reliable. This proved to be the case, for when fitted to the P3 Grand Prix car, it notched up at least forty major successes between 1932 and 1935. Most notable of these was probably Nuvolari's victory at the Nurburgring in 1935 against the mighty German 'Silver Arrows'.

By way of counter-attacking the Mercedes-Benz and Auto Unions, Scuderia Ferrari introduced the fearsome twin-engined Bimotore in 1935, which used two P3 engines mounted one behind and one in front of the driver. He sat on top of a three-speed gearbox that drove the rear wheels. The car was capable of 200mph (320kph) in a straight line, but a ravenous appetite for tyres marked it down as a failure.

Meanwhile, in the corporate world, things were not going well for the company financially. Ownership passed from the Banco di Sconto into government receivership and

A powerful ingredient of the Alfa Romeo attraction is its sporting pedigree, exemplified by the 6C 1750 Zagato-bodied Gran Sport, produced between 1929 and 1933. On the left is a 101-series Giulia Spider of 1962, which sustained the tradition.

Alfa Romeo was refloated with its sights set on more diverse commercial markets, including trucks, coaches and marine and aircraft engines. Cars for the domestic market took the form of handsome but hardly outstanding four-door saloons, powered by a straight-six engine of 1900cc or 2300cc.

During the post-war period, Alfa Romeo manufactured a variety of vehicles, such as the mid-'50s Romeo 2 van, in this case converted into an ambulance. It was front-wheel drive, powered by a rearward-facing Giulietta engine mated by a driveshaft to a four-speed ZF transaxle. Alongside is a 101-series Giulietta Berlina.

This sleek 6C 2500 cabriolet was built in 1951 by Touring-of-Milan, who probably clad more of these chassis than any of the other coach-builders of the period, and most notably the Villa d'Este coupe of 1950.

The 6C 2300's box-section chassis was considerably lighter than the C-section girders of its 8C 2300 predecessor, and its performance was sufficient to satisfy a demand which could keep the factory going as a commercial proposition. Short-wheelbase sports chassis were offered with bodies made by Zagato, Stabilimenti Farina (Pinin's elder brother Giovanni's company), Castagna and Touring-of-Milan. Three coupé versions with Touring coachwork took the first three places in a 24-hour race at Pescara, and one such came fourth in the 1937 Mille Miglia. Alfa successes in this fabulous event were legion. With the exception of 1931, one or other type of Alfa won it outright from 1928 to 1938. Most notable were the

The six-cylinder 6C 3000 CM sports racing car of 1953 used a long-stroke version of the 1900 four-cylinder engine. Only four coupés and two spiders were built, and Juan-Manuel Fangio drove one of the open cars to victory in the Supercortemaggiore Grand Prix of 1954.

8C 2900As, which took the first three places in 1936.

By the end of the decade though, production vehicles were leaving the factory at a trickle. Under Mussolini's direction, the main thrust of the company's automotive efforts was to be seen to match the German cars on the Grand Prix circuit, and Alfa Romeo's role bore much the same responsibility for national pride then as Ferrari's does today.

Still bent on outdoing the Germans, Jano's last creation for Alfa's Scuderia Ferrari racing team, before he left in a fit of self-deprecation to join Lancia in 1937 – and subsequently Ferrari – was the twin-supercharged V12 model. It produced 430bhp, which proved to be more than the rear axle could cope with, and in the wake of this failure, Alfa lost the services of the man who had been perhaps their greatest asset.

Other engine designs were pressed into service, including the 3.0-litre V16 – an extended version of the V12 – which managed second place in the 1938 Italian Grand Prix. The wide-angle V12 engine was tried in the Tipo 162, and the mid-mounted flat-twelve in the all-independent suspension Tipo 512. Development of this highly promising car was stalled by the start of the Second World War.

Derivatives of the Giulia Sprint GT were raced extensively in international events and at club level. This is Dave Hood's highly modified 2000 GTV club racer in the paddock at Castle Combe in 1988. Most of the panels are in glass fibre.

This sports-racing Alfa Romeo is a 1900 Sport Spider, built in 1954. Note the four-leaf clover – quadri-foglio – competition decal and twin exhaust pipes exiting from the sill. Rear suspension features a DeDion axle and in-board drum brakes. It has also been referred to as the 2000 Sportiva. Only two Sport Spiders and two coupés were built, and examples can be seen at the Alfa Romeo museum at Arese.

BIRTH OF THE ALFETTA

Before hostilities began, Teutonic victories on the Grand Prix circuit had become so predictable that the race promoters introduced the voiturette class as an entertaining diversion. This category was rather like Formula 3000 or perhaps Formula 3 today, serving as a curtain-raiser for the main event, and as such was hotly contested. It turned out to be the salvation of Alfa Romeo's morale as well as its prestige, as they found instant success with the single-supercharger straight-eight Tipo 158 Alfettas. These elegant racers with all-independent suspension were designed by Gioacchino Columbo, whose supercharged 1.5-litre V8 engines were based on one half of the V16 unit. They finished first and second on their debut at Livorno in 1938, but they would really come into their own in the post-war Grand Prix era, when they were virtually unbeatable.

Nicola Romeo died on 15 August 1938, and thus was spared witnessing the devastation of his company's Portello factory. Its workforce of 8,500 had been involved in the Italian war effort, and, as a consequence, the factory was a natural target for Allied bombing raids. The factory was hit twice in

25

The spartan cockpit of the 1900 Sport Spider clearly indicates competition usage, surrounded by low, wrap-around windscreen, with a single bucket seat, and miscellaneous dials scattered across the dashboard.

1943 and again in 1944. Despite these apparently major setbacks, production of aero and marine engines was maintained, and the racing programme resumed with the 1.5-litre Tipo 158 almost the moment peace was declared.

Five Alfettas had been secretly hidden away during the war years, and afterwards development continued under chief designer Orazio Satta. The 158 and its derivative, the 420bhp 159, recorded no fewer than 47 wins from 54 Grands Prix, making it the most successful GP car of all time. Alfa Romeo 158/9s achieved complete supremacy in the post-war years, up to 1951. Giuseppe 'Nino' Farina won the first ever Formula 1 World Championship with a 158 in 1950, and

A number of soft-top derivatives were built by the leading Italian carrozzerie *on the 1900 floorpan, like this 1957 Zagato Spider. The lines are not so dissimilar to those of the smaller Pininfarina-styled Giulietta.*

State-of-the-art welding gear in use at Portello in the 1950s, tack-welding the longitudinal members onto the underside of a Giulietta floor-pan.

Juan-Manuel Fangio's Alfa beat the Ferraris of Alberto Ascari and Froilan Gonzales to the title in 1951.

When production resumed after the war, Alfa Romeo made a variety of vehicles and components, from stylish buses and coaches, horseboxes and trucks of different configurations, to aircraft engines and static industrial diesel engines. The company even made fashionable domestic ovens. There was still a demand for grand and stylish cars, however, and one of the most imposing was the 2500 Super Sport Freccia d'Oro, which appeared in 1947. Although its mechanical specification was designed before the war, it illustrated the course on which Alfa Romeo was set. Its straight-six, 2,443cc twin-cam engine developed 105bhp and drove through a four-speed all-synchromesh gearbox, which was operated by a lever on the steering column. The advanced aerodynamic two-door factory-built saloon body was welded to the chassis, paving the way for the successful stress-bearing structure of the future. Saloon versions of the 2500 Super Sport could seat five, with the curious layout of three in the front and two in the rear. Alfas have often been versatile, and a Freccia d'Oro even competed in the 1950 Carrera Panamericana. True to form, there were also elegant coupé and cabriolet versions, built on the chassis of the 2500 Super Sport by

The four-cylinder 1900 engine, circa 1957, showing the slanted cam covers, rearward distributor and sump location.

Giulietta Berlinas being prepared for painting on the labour-intensive Portello production line.

Carrozzerie such as Pinin Farina, Touring, Castagna and Boneschi.

RACE CRED

When the regulations for Formula 1 cars changed, and in the face of increasing successes by Ferrari, Alfa Romeo withdrew from the Grand Prix scene. They did not return to that particular arena until 1970, when they provided V8 engines for the up-and-coming McLaren and March teams. A 3.0-litre flat-twelve engine was fitted to one of Graham Hill's Lolas in 1975, but was taken up by Brabham the following year.

Both Bertone and Pinin Farina were commissioned to provide proposals for the Giulietta Spider. This is Bertone's offering, similar to his Arnolt Bristol roadster and also drawing on his 2000 Sportiva coupé prototype of 1954. It was not selected, largely because Bertone was heavily involved with Sprint production and Alfa wished to involve another coachbuilder.

Alfa Romeo 105-Series Spider bodyshells in the final stages of assembly at the Pininfarina plant, in tandem with Peugeot 504 Coupés, which along with Fiat Dinos and 124 Spiders, were also made at the Grugliasco factory.

Brabham continued with Alfa flat-twelve and V-12 engines for four seasons, until 1979, when Alfa Romeo themselves came out with the flat-twelve-powered Tipo 177. For 1980, hopes rested on the V-12 Tipo 179 and 180, raced by Bruno Giacomelli, Vittorio Brambilla and Andrea de Cesaris; tragically, Patrick Depailler lost his life in a test session at Hockenheim. By the year's end Giacomelli was able to qualify his car on pole position, so the potential was certainly there. However, in the five subsequent years, Alfa Romeo's Formula 1 effort reaped little success, even with former World Champion Mario Andretti on the strength. There was no joy in 1981, largely because the team was unprepared at the beginning of the season for the ban on slid-

ing skirts as aerodynamic aids, and experiments with different suspension systems to make up the deficit proved unsuccessful. Highlights of this otherwise luckless period included the reappearance in 1982 of the Tipo 179 with a 1.5-litre turbocharged V8, and de Cesaris leading the Belgian Grand Prix at Spa for 18 laps in 1983. Riccardo Patrese and Eddie Cheever drove Tipo 184Ts in 1984 with the cars resplendent in the bright green livery of Benetton fashions, but they were seldom on the pace, and even managed to collide with each other on the first lap at Kyalami in 1985. Under something of a cloud, Alfa Romeo withdrew from Formula 1 at the end of the year.

Any car manufacturer who participates in motor sport, whether as a publicity-

Production of the 105-series cars began at the new Arese plant in north-west Milan in 1962, and this aerial shot taken a decade later shows the administration and museum block in the right foreground.

seeking exercise or to 'improve the breed' has its reputation bolstered to a great extent, provided there are at least some successes. And if the 1980s represented something of a nadir in Alfa Romeo's sporting heritage, its credibility as a maker of production-line models was also tarnished at the same time by the rust crisis. It was not alone, as the corrosion syndrome also hit Lancia and Fiat. It began during the 1970s, and seems to have been the legacy of using adulterated Eastern-block steel. Possibly what carried the company through these troubled times was the enduring support of a hard-core of enthusiasts who continued to buy and use Alfa products. These people remembered the halcyon days of the late twenties and early thirties, and the post-war Grand Prix domination. Younger people recalled the heady days of the sixties, when the little GT-Z coupés and the Giulia Sprint GTA and its derivatives were invincible in their classes in sports and touring car races. Alfa Romeo's participation in motor sport has

seemed to ebb and flow with waves of corporate enthusiasm. In sports car racing, things never seemed quite so gloomy as the 1979–85 Formula 1 debacle, although perhaps Alfa Romeo lacked the consistency, commitment and even the administrational aptitude of Ferrari.

SPORTS, GT AND TOURING CAR COMPETITION

Having dropped out of Formula 1 at the end of the 1951 season, Alfa Romeo spent the next two years campaigning the purposeful Colli-bodied 6C 3000CM Disco Volante sports cars, which Fangio drove to second place in the 1953 Mille Miglia and Le Mans events. The graduation to mass production in the early 1950s allowed many more private owners to go racing in events like the Mille Miglia, Giro D'Italia and the Carrera Messicana. They entered with their 1900 saloons, Bertone-styled Giulietta Sprints and SSs, Zagato-bodied SZ coupés, and Pininfarina spiders, and there were very many successes at this level.

The factory built a 'monoposto' Giulietta Spider prototype that had a plexiglass wrap-around windshield and metal tonneau over the passenger seat. It first appeared at the Giro di Sicilia on 7 April 1956, and later the same month it was driven in the Mille Miglia by Alfa's test driver Consalvo Sanesi. However, he crashed when the gearbox seized. That was that, as far as works Spiders were concerned, and instead, development went into the Giulietta Sprint Veloce and the privately run SVZ and SZs.

Alfa Romeo management started to take racing seriously again in 1964, and bought

up Carlo Chiti's Autodelta Racing Team, which formed the basis for virtually all works competition activity until 1985. Most of Autodelta's victories were achieved in the mid-to-late sixties with the achingly beautiful Giulia GT-Z coupés in long-distance GT and sports prototype racing, and the GTA coupés in production car events. The GTA was the lightweight version of the Giulia Sprint GT, and its derivatives the GT Am and GTA Junior scooped their classes in the European Touring Car Championship in 1966, '67, '70, and were outright winners of the title in 1971 and '72. The 2000 GTV versions regularly won the King's Cup team prize in the

Hard to say who stars in this strangely composed Alfa publicity shot of the Giulia Super, which provided the floorpan and mechanicals for the 105-series Spiders. Which one would you like in your garage?

The first 101-series car was the Sprint Speciale, which had an entirely new bodyshell drawn by Franco Scaglione for Bertone, and its curvaceous coupé shape was based on the Giulietta floorpan.

Spa-Francorchamps 24-Hour race. I dwell on these competition successes, because of course the classic 105-series Spiders are directly related to the Sprint GT and GTV, and as such benefited in quite a direct way from the mechanical improvements which derived from the competition activity.

The Alfa which contested the sports-prototype category was a different animal altogether: the fragile Tipo 33 first raced in 1967 with almost no success whatsoever, and to some enthusiasts it seemed a pity that Autodelta had abandoned the TZ2 and GTA projects to concentrate on apparently fruitless sports-prototype events. The mid-engined 2.0-litre V8 held considerable potential, however, and Tipo 33/2s finished well up in events like the BOAC 500km at Brands Hatch, the Targa Florio, and Le Mans in 1968. But not until 1971 did reliability and performance improve sufficiently for the 3.0-litre V8-engined 33/3 to notch up some meaningful successes, including victory in the BOAC race and the Targa Florio. With sports car racing dominated by Ferrari and then Matra over the following two seasons, Autodelta had to be content with just a handful of placings. Then with very little works opposition, the flat-twelve 33/TT 12 had more or less everything its own way in 1975, and again in 1977, although without top-class competition the World Championship victories were rather hollow ones.

FROM 1900 TO GIULIETTA TO GIULIA

Cars like the Freccia d'Oro were bought by the motoring élite, but the first Alfa Romeo sports car to be accessible to a wider public was the 1900 Super Sprint Coupé of 1954. This streamlined two-plus-two was derived from the 1900 saloon of 1950, and powered by the four-cylinder 1,975cc unit. Prominent among its styling cues was the three-lobed front grille and the unusual up-turned trapezoidal rear window. The design borrowed a number of elements from the previous 6C 2500 'Villa d'Este', which were also echoed in the contemporary cabriolet by Pinin Farina.

The 1900 Super Sprint relied for its performance on its good power-to-weight ratio, as its bodywork was exceptionally light. The *Superleggera*, or Superlight, construction method was the speciality of coachbuilders Touring-of-Milan, based on the use of hand beaten aluminium sheet, stapled to a frame of small steel pipes and tubes welded together and built up on the floorpan.

1750 Berlina bodyshells go down the line at Arese in 1967. A line of step-front Giulia Sprint GTs can be seen to the left.

In 1951, when it commissioned Carrozzeria Touring to design the coupé version of the 1900 Super Sprint, Alfa Romeo also engaged Pinin Farina to create a convertible version. The brief was to reflect the company's typical styling, incorporating in particular the three-lobe front grille, because both models would be on sale at Alfa Romeo dealerships.

The development of the coupé and cabriolet posed considerable engineering problems, as the days of the backbone chassis were over with the advent of the 1900 saloon's stress-bearing unit-construction body. They had to utilize its steel floorpan, and the project entailed an enormous amount of engineering design work to create a suitably stiff frame.

Two successive series of the 1900 Cabriolet were built up to 1958, with Sprint (1,884 cc and 100bhp engine) and Super Sprint (1,975cc, 115bhp) mechanicals.

After the 1900 series, which established the company as a maker of mass-produced cars, the next phase in Alfa Romeo's evolution as a major manufacturer was the Giulietta range. With the company in state ownership, the government organised a lottery to generate the funds to make the tooling and plant to produce the Giulietta saloon. The idea was that holders of the winning share certificates would win new cars. However, the draw came, and no cars had yet been built. In order to stave off the inevitable outcry, the up-and-coming coach-builder Nuccio Bertone was commissioned to turn his Giulietta Sprint coupé prototype into a production reality. The prize must now have exceeded the lottery winners' wildest dreams.

The Giulietta Sprint was powered by Orazio Satta's 1300 twin-cam, and launched to much acclaim at the 1954 Turin Motor Show, and Bertone and his design engineer Franco Scaglione continued to

Alfa shield 'radiator grille' on this 1978 Spider 2000 Veloce conforms to corporate identity of the period, similar to contemporary late-'70s Alfetta series models. Company logo consists of a red cross – the arms of the City of Milan – combined with the Visconti family's medieval shield adornment of a serpent devouring a child.

produce the cars by hand at the rate of about four a day. Until this point, it had not been Alfa's intention to make a small grand touring car on a mass-produced basis, but demand was such that Bertone himself – yet to hit the big-time – was obliged to gear up for limited mass-production. Up till now, the only mass-produced item on the car was the grille, sourced from the Romeo van parts bin.

It is most unusual for a GT version of a particular model range to precede the bread-and-butter saloons, but production of the 750-series Giulietta 750C Berlina was under way by 1955. The Spider was introduced the same year, with higher-performance twin-Weber carb Veloce versions of the Sprint and Spider following in 1956. The TI version of the Berlina came out in

1957, when 8,940 units of the saloon were built, and improved longer-wheelbase versions of the Sprint and Spider arrived in 1959, by which time Bertone was turning out up to 34 Sprints a day.

Before the Spider got the go-ahead, prototypes were invited from Bertone, whose offering was redolent of the Sportiva and directly comparable with his design for the Arnolt-Bristol, and from Pinin Farina. The latter had produced fine coachwork for the 6C 2500 and 1900 models, and came up with three prototypes for the Giulietta sports car including one with Cadillac-style bumper overriders. As Pinin Farina was in a position to tool up for 20 new Spiders a day, and with Bertone fully engaged on Sprints, Pinin Farina got the contract.

The evolution of the 1300cc Giulietta Spiders unfolds in the next chapter, and we see how the 750- and 101-series models – Normale and Veloce – metamorphose almost imperceptibly into the 101-series 1600cc Giulia Spider of 1962, which, apart from its bonnet 'air-scoop', looked almost identical. The same mechanicals, with the addition of a fifth gear, were carried over into the newly styled successor, known as the Duetto.

Launched in 1966, this 105-series Pininfarina Spider epitomized wind-in-the-hair freedom for a newly wealthy generation. By this time, production facilities had moved from the Portello factory, restricted as it was from further development by a housing estate, to a new factory complex at Arese on the outskirts of Milan. The company's three-mile (4.8km) Balocco test track near Turin was opened the following year in 1964.

Just as the Giulietta Berlina and Sprint models were marketed alongside the

The 116-series Alfetta range began life in 1973, culminating in the 2.5-litre fuel-injected GTV6 that was in production from 1981 to 1987. It won the British Touring Car title in 1983, and the author is seen attempting to emulate this feat in his own car at Snetterton's Russell bend in 1990.

Spider, so the Duetto and its successors shared the Alfa Romeo showrooms with the Berlina and Sprint GT derivatives, the TI and Super four-door saloons and the coupé-bodied GTV touring cars. The more staid-looking 1750 and 2000cc Berlinas replaced the fluted and scalloped Giulia saloons in 1967, only to be superseded themselves by the Alfetta range in 1972. There has always been a period of up to two years' overlap on the production lines, where the incoming and outgoing models are produced side by side, and although there is thus no clearly defined cut-off point, there is some merit in hedging your bets with an extended production run. Attracted by government incentives and the prospect of cheap labour, Alfa Romeo commenced production of the Alfasud at its Pomigliano d'Arco commercial vehicle plant near Naples. Despite appalling labour relations problems at Pomigliano, the Sprint derivative of this excellent little car was still being built in 1988. The Alfasud's successor, the 33, was made there too, although the Sportwagon estate version was built by Pininfarina up at Grugliasco near Turin.

However, despite its undoubted qualities, the Alfasud had cost Alfa Romeo dearly, and an attempt to head off financial disaster was made in 1980 by embarking on a joint venture with Nissan to produce an Alfasud-powered Nissan Cherry, marketed as the Arna. It was not a success in sales terms, and the venture ended.

The late 1970s was not a good time for Alfa Romeo. In 1977 the company's losses totalled $148.5m against sales of $1.1bn, and the cumulative deficit for the previous five years was $670m. This translated into a loss of $1K per car. With accounts like these, venture capital was impossible to access. Yet despite the fact that the new line at Arese was running at two-thirds capacity, the Alfetta range was augmented

With the launch of the 156 four-door saloon in 1997, Alfa Romeo's fortunes looked set to rise anew. With in-house styling by Centro Stile, the 156 embodied many of the company's traditional hallmarks, and like its other saloon models, it was available with a choice of power-units.

in November 1977 by the new Giulietta saloon, something of a gamble in the light of the company's dire financial plight. Bizarrely, production and distribution of the new model was hindered by Red Brigade terrorist attacks. Just how serious they were was demonstrated by the assassination of Christian Democrat leader Aldo Moro in 1978.

The last evolution of the Giugiaro-styled Alfetta range was the GTV6 coupé, introduced in 1980, which used the six-cylinder engine from the large Alfa 6 saloon, and enjoyed consistent success as a class winner in European touring car racing in the early-to-mid 1980s. It was feats like these that maintained a core of interest and commitment to Alfa's fortunes.

Probably the most momentous occasion in Alfa Romeo's corporate history took place in 1987, when Fiat took control. With its future now relatively secure, Alfa began to rise with confidence from the fairly miserable circumstances of the 1980s. New model ranges included the Alfa 75 saloon, named (or rather, numbered) to celebrate the company's three-quarters of a century in business, the elegant Pininfarina-designed 164, and by the turn of the decade, the 75's successor, the front-wheel-drive 155 saloon had arrived. The Zagato-built SZ ES30 coupé appeared in 1990, a pugnacious beast if ever there was one, based on the platform and running gear of the 3.0-litre Alfa 75. And last but not least, the long-lived Spider was given a proper facelift in 1990.

Alfa's flagship, the 164 saloon, shared the same floorpan as the so-called Type Four cars – the technical consortium which spawned the Lancia Thema, Fiat Croma and Saab 9000 – and the Alfa 164's Pininfarina styling outshone that of its rather dowdy cousins. Unfortunately, Peugeot stole some of its thunder when it brought out its very similar Pininfarina commission, the 405, ahead of the Alfa, much to Milan's chagrin. These big front-wheel drive 164 executive saloons were available with three engine options, the 3.0-litre V6, 2.0-litre Twin-spark and diesel.

The range progressed on all fronts with the launch of the all-new Spider and GTV models in 1995, followed soon afterwards by the compact 145 three-door hatch and 146 five-door saloon. Alfa Romeo's current *piece de resistance*, the 156, was launched in 1997 at Frankfurt, and by the time you read this, I could well have put down a deposit on one! It looks that good. But hold on, you are thinking. Isn't this book meant to be eulogising Spiders? Well yes, but the 156's practical benefits complement its excellent good looks, and for the time being that swings the balance in this household.

18 months after its UK launch, the Spider took pole position on the Alfa Romeo stand at Earls Court despite the presence of the new 156. Tipler negotiates a test drive with Alfa GB press officer Huguette Boyagis, while Fiat Corporate Communications Officer Bob Hoare (left), looks on sceptically.

2   Evolution of the Spider

THE DUETTO'S ANCESTORS

The model commonly perceived as the classic Alfa Romeo Spider is the 105-series car, derived from the Duetto of 1966. However, the previous range of Spiders is of equal, if not greater importance, because of the technological leap it made in redefining contemporary sports car standards in the 1950s. Basically, these were the 750- and 101-series Giulietta and Giulia Spiders, all powered by Dott.

Orazio Satta Puliga's enduring all-alloy twin-cam engine, with seemingly illogical overlaps in specifications, names and numbers. The 750- and 101- designations refer to chassis numbering, although 750-Series cars, confusingly, have chassis numbers beginning 1495 (750 was the factory number that was originally applied to a front-wheel-drive mini-Berlina project, which came to nothing). More logically, 101-series Spider chassis numbers start 10123.

Well-known Pininfarina publicity shot – but nonetheless one of the best – of one of the three prototypes for the 750-series Giulietta Spider. Chrome intake surrounds and door handles are absent here, and quarter-light windows were omitted on production cars.

The dashboard of this Pininfarina prototype 750-series Giulietta was given a less sporting steering wheel than the production models. The dashboard is more austere, and the central dial has its own pinnacle, rather than all three dials being covered by a single hood.

Giulietta Spiders were in production as 750- and 101-series cars from 1955 to 1962, when the bonnet was altered slightly and the engine bored and stroked from 1300 (1290cc) to 1600 (1570cc), and it metamorphosed accordingly into the 101-series Giulia Spider. This car remained in production until 1965, and was superseded by the Duetto.

What all these cars have in common are bodies styled by Pininfarina. Carrozzeria Pininfarina has designed the shape of most Ferraris, including classics such as the 275GTB4, the 365B Daytona and the F40, as well as a raft of far more prosaic tin-tops, like the finned family cars of the 1950s and most Peugeots since. But the cars that really made the firm's reputation in the fifties and early sixties were the Alfa Romeo 750-series Giulietta and 101-series Giulia Spiders.

THE 750-SERIES SPIDER

Evolution of the Duetto's forerunners is complicated. I referred to Evan Wilson's book *Alfa Romeo Giulietta* when writing this chapter, as he is thoroughly dialled-in on specification changes to all the various 750- and 101-series models. It is also worth mentioning the Hughes/Da Prato book *Veloce* here, which is informative and entertaining on the competition history of the contemporary Giulietta Sprint, Sprint Speciale and Sprint Zagato models. There are also a few books available on Giulias, including Richard Bremner's, which deals with the Coupé and Spider, and my own book, which is about the Sprint GT and GTA.

As well as the Bertone prototype, Alfa Romeo commissioned examples from Pininfarina, who made three Giulietta Spiders before the design was finally signed off. The

Giovan Battista Farina

The man we have to thank for three generations of Alfa Spiders was born Giovan Battista Farina in Turin in 1895. His nickname was Pinin, or 'little boy', and it stuck, so much so that aged 60, he changed his name by deed poll to Pininfarina. Thus anything designed or built before 1955 should be referred to as 'Pinin Farina', and anything after that date is 'Pininfarina'.

Having worked for his brother Giovanni for 20 years at the Stabilimenti Farina coachworks, Pinin set up his own in 1930. He was actually offered a job by Henry Ford during the tough years of the 1930s, when he would go to the United States to keep abreast of trends in the motor industry. Pinin's first design was a Lancia DiLambda, executed in 1932, and this was followed by commissions from Fiat and Lancia, with an exercise on a Bentley chassis as well. Pinin's first post-war creation was the Cisitalia 202 coupé, its tubular-frame chassis powered by an 1100cc Fiat engine (considered by New York's Museum of Modern Art to be worth a place in its Salon of Influential Car Design).

Apart from all the classic Ferrari designs, from 250 GT and 275 GTB4, to 365B Daytona and, right up to date, the Testarossa and F40, consultancy work during the period we are mostly concerned with here, the fifties and sixties, produced ranges of family cars like the finned Lancias, Peugeots and Austin Cambridges. But of the styling exercises carried out during the fifties, there is one in particular which can be regarded as the harbinger of the Duetto.

In 1956, Pininfarina acquired one of the 6C 3000CM sports racers, which Juan Manuel Fangio had driven to second place in the Mille Miglia and Le Mans events in 1953. These fabulous cars were originally bodied by Colli who, paradoxically, also made the Giulietta Giardinetta estates and a handful of stretched Berlina limos, but Pininfarina rebodied this car no less than four times for different motor shows. These evolutionary prototypes were known as the Super Flow series, and to some extent all contained styling cues which would surface almost a decade later in the Duetto. Another showpiece, known as Superfast III, which appeared at the 1961 Turin Show, was presumed to have been Pininfarina's answer to the Nuccio Bertone-designed Sprint Speciale of 1959, a concept which emanated from Bertone's legendary BAT series. Whatever the motives, the Pininfarina show car bore the scalloped flanks, rounded tail, and similar frontal treatment and wheel arches which were to reappear in the Duetto.

Much of the styling at Pininfarina during the 1950s and '60s was done by Pinin's son Sergio and son-in-law Renzo Carli, and they continued to run the business from 1959, assuming complete control immediately after Pinin's death in 1966. The Pininfarina firm is now controlled by Paulo and Andrea, the third generation of the family. Despite setbacks like the fire of 1989, the classic Alfa Romeo Spiders have always been built in part or as a whole at Pininfarina's Grugliasco factory near Turin.

Pinin Farina's rather heavy coachwork on this 1947 6C 2500 cabriolet is typical of the period. The bonnet has an unusual centre hinge arrangement, and like most luxury cars of the day it was made in right-hand drive.

first couple lacked wind-up side windows and, claims Wilson, the third one was equipped with wind-up windows following discussions with US importer Max Hoffman (that name again) of the Hoffman Motor Car Company. He told Alfa Romeo management that the cars would do better in the States if they had 'roll-up' windows. Indeed, his prognosis that the Spiders would do well in the US – better than the Sprints – was proved correct by an excellent response in the marketplace. The second prototype was also finished with a column shift and curious Cadillac-style bullet-shaped bumper overriders.

The regular 750-series Spiders were designated 'Normale', and were in production from 1955 to 1959. They were powered by the 1290cc cast aluminium in-line four-cylinder twin-cam, driving through a four-speed gearbox. Suspension was by double A-arm (wishbones), ball joints, coil springs and Girling dampers, and an anti-roll bar at the front, with longitudinal radius arms, triangular lateral locator, coil springs and dampers. Alfin drum brakes were fitted all round.

The cars' bodies were built at the Pininfarina factory, and the panels that made up the monocoque shells were stamped out on conventional dies and progressively butt-welded together. External seams were either eliminated or accentuated, and the relatively shallow and uncomplicated profile of the panels helped keep the shell rigid yet lightweight. Not only was the design sophisticated, but there were wind-up windows at a time when the likes of MG and Triumph were still offering side screens and canvas flaps above the doors for access and making hand signals.

It was soon clear that the Giulietta package was capable of handling and delivering more performance, and indeed, enthusiasts demanded it. So in 1956 the uprated Spider

Slanted scalloped flutings, rear wheel arch spats and the shark's fins give the Pininfarina Super Flow 1957 show car a nose-up stance. There are some similarities with Boano's 1956 Super Sprint, but already some of the styling cues of the Duetto are evident, a decade before its launch.

and Sprint versions gained the 'Veloce' – or 'Fast' – tag, and the Berlina was offered in TI – Turismo Internazionale – form. The Spider Veloce model was now the 750F, and for a short time it was marketed as the 'Super Spider'.

Veloce modifications included a major reworking of the 1300 twin-cam, employing twin sidedraught Weber DCO3 carburettors instead of a single downdraught Solex, fitting a high-compression head and high-lift cams, four-branch manifold and a finned alloy sump containing a built-in oil cooler. These alterations conspired to lift the power from 65 to 90bhp, but the Veloce

models were not without problems. Being more highly strung, they had a healthy appetite for spark plugs, which could easily foul-up at low revs in traffic, they did not care for low-octane fuel – let alone unleaded – and the sump was such an efficient engine cooler that the heater was almost useless. The Veloce Spider needed to be revved hard to extract maximum performance, and was capable of going right up to 8,000rpm, well in excess of the 6,500rpm red line. The Giulietta Normales all had the column gearshift so common in the mid-fifties, which could be operated fairly swiftly, but was less slick than the transmission tunnel-mounted change with which Veloce models were fitted. By 1959, a new transmission had virtually eliminated the second-gear selection problems that had afflicted the earlier cars. The Veloce cars also received the Weber DCOE carburettors, which was also considered to be an improvement.

The Giulietta's short wheelbase produced an excellent ride, with handling far superior to the rest of the sports car herd, and its suspension set up proved that an independent rear-end was not essential. High-speed adjustments of line through corners could be made by subtle pressure on the accelerator pedal to counteract understeer. 'Protagonists of all-independent suspension must find it difficult to decry the Spyder's [sic] live rear axle and coil springing', said *The Autocar* magazine in 1959.

These days we tend to scoff at drum brakes, but the Giulietta's 10.5-inch Alfins were not only very effective, they were a work of art. Made of cast aluminium with external fins and iron inserts, they had cast aluminium shoes and were stamped *sinestra* and *destro* for right and left. They helped make the fast, agile 750-series Giulietta Spider Veloce a match on the open road for most of the larger-engined 1950s sports cars.

As production increased, the company underwent quite serious internal reorganisation as it metamorphosed from a relatively small specialist producer to a serious, if not quite a major manufacturer. The cars themselves had to comply with World-market criteria, and not just with European standards, which in any case varied slightly from country to country: for

The Giulia Spider's hardtop provides excellent rear vision, and complements the styling well enough. This 101-series car's larger rear light clusters can be seen.

Alfa Romeo Giulietta Spider (1955–62)

Layout	Monocoque construction, Pininfarina-designed and -built two-seater soft-top
Engine	
Type	Four cylinders in line, front-mounted
Block	Cast aluminium with slip-fit cast-iron cylinder liners, Mahle pistons
Head	Cast alumininium, cross-flow, hemispherical chambers
Bore and stroke	77 x 75mm = 1290cc (3 x 2.9in = 77.4cu.in)
Valves	Two per cylinder, inclined overhead valves. Bucket tappets, shim adjustment
Camshafts	Twin overhead, chain driven from the crankshaft
Drive	Rear-wheel drive
Power output	65bhp at 6,100rpm (Veloce: 90 bhp at 6,500rpm)
Compression ratio	8.5:1 (Veloce: 9.1:1)
Induction	Single down-draught Solex carburettor (Veloce: two side-draught twin-choke Webers)
Generator	750-series: Marelli DN44A. 101-series: Bosch LJ/GEG200/12/2700R
Regulator	750-series: Marelli IR32A. 101-series: Bosch RS/VA200/12A2
Starter	750-series: Marelli MT35E. 101-series: Bosch AL/EEFo.7/12R11
Distributor	750-series: Marelli S71B. 101-series: Bosch VJU4BR41MK
Coil	750-series: Marelli B17A. 101-series: Bosch TK12A3
Spark Plugs	750-series: Marelli CW225G (Veloce: CNW1000B) 101-series: Spica-Lodge 2HLNG (Veloce: Spica-Lodge RL47)
Transmission	
Type	4-speed manual, Porsche-type synchromesh, aluminium split case
Clutch	Single disc with coil-spring pressure plate, divided prop shaft with front Metalastic joint, double universal joint, slip spline, central support bearing; hypoid rear axle
Ratios	Normale: 4th, 1:1.00; 3rd, 1:1.357; 2nd, 1:1.985; 1st, 1:3.258; reverse, 1:3.252. Final drive: 9:41 (Veloce: 10:41)
Performance	
Acceleration	0–60mph (0–100km/h): 14.8sec. (Veloce: 11.0sec)
Maximum speed	102.5mph (164km/h) (Veloce: 111.8mph (178.8km/h))
Fuel consumption	25mpg (11.32ltr/100km) urban cycle, 30mpg (9.4ltr/100km) touring, 27.5mpg(10.3ltr/100km) overall
Suspension and Steering	
Front	Independent by coil springs, wishbones and dampers, anti-roll bar
Rear	Live axle, longitudinal radius arms, transverse link, coil springs and dampers
Wheels and tyres	Bolt-on steel 15 x 4.5in rims, 155-15 tyres
Brakes	Alfin drums all round

Dimensions

Wheelbase: 750-series: 7ft 2in (2.196m) 101-series: 7ft 3in (2.250m)

Front track: 4ft 2in (1.292m) 101-series: 4ft 2.5in (1.292m)

Rear track   4ft 1in (1.270m)

Weight: 750-series: 1,907lb (860kg) 101-series: 1,951lb (885kg)

Fuel tank capacity   11.66gal (53ltr)

Production

Produced 1955–62 (Veloce introduced 1956)

Quantity 6,381 units of Normale 750-Series,

368 units of Veloce 750-Series,

10,579 units of Normale 101-Series,

1,911 units of Veloce 101-Series

This 101-series Giulietta Spider is fitted with wire-spoke wheels, an unusual option which lends a certain lightness to the design.

example, German 'Spyders' were the only ones to have sun visors fitted. Unavailability of right-hand-drive cars made Giuliettas a rarity in Britain, Australia and New Zealand. While Berlinas and a few Sprints were imported into the UK in right-hand drive-format from 1961, the Giulietta Spider was never produced with right-hand drive. In South Africa they had to make do with right-hand-drive Berlinas in CKD form and build them there. The US market posed slightly different demands, even in the mid-fifties. For some reason, US Spiders could not have flashing indicators.

By the late-fifties, Alfa Romeo and its suppliers of components were looking at ways to improve the Giulietta series, and by 1959 the uprated cars were in production. These were the 101-series cars, whose mechanical specification was altered quite subtly in almost every respect, from crankcase dimensions to cylinder head height right down to valve guides and cam followers. A number of interim cars were assembled using a combination of components from both sides of the model changeover, and was something that came to be regarded by Alfa enthusiasts as par for the course. While the company never quoted any performance increase, it was agreed at the time among the Alfisti that power-output of the Normale models had risen from 65bhp to 80bhp. Speeds in the gears were 51mph (82kph) in second, 74mph (119kph) in third, and 96mph (154kph) in top, with a delay in accomplishing the last 5mph (8kph). Smooth driving could achieve 30mpg (9.4/100km)

The rotund little SZ was a successful competition car, produced between 1959 and 1961. Its lightweight Zagato body was powered by the 1300 Giulietta Veloce engine with five-speed gearbox. Predictably, it was austere inside, and was shod with 15in Campagnolo Elektron alloy wheels.

from the 11.5-gallon (52.2-litre) fuel tank, although if the car was driven as it should be, the figure went down to 20mpg (14.15/100km). List price for the Normale in 1959 was £2,091 in the UK.

The critics smiled on the Giulietta too. In December 1959, *The Autocar* magazine commented on its long-term test car that: 'There is no more desirable sports car; it sets standards of performance, handling and refinement that very few others can match. The steering is light, precise and the car responds to the slightest touch of the wheel. There is scarcely any roll or tyre squeal when cornering, and the driver at once feels confident about taking corners very fast indeed.' They went on to say that: 'The ride is an excellent compromise between firmness for high speeds and sufficient resilience to avoid bumps and shakes on poor road surfaces.' But, they pointed out, 'Ground clearance is marginal, particularly for rally work.' The big drum brakes, they said, 'were smooth in operation, reasonably light and showed no signs of fading during bursts of fast driving. The balance, front and rear, seemed good, there being no premature rear-wheel locking.'

Almost forty years on, it is interesting to note the aspects that *Autocar's* testers commented on. Reporting on the Giulietta's flexibility, they said: 'In traffic, it will potter, snatch-free, in top gear at under 20mph, and pull away without signs of distress. This speed represents no more than 1,100rpm.'

Writing about the design of the car, *Autocar* said: 'It is commendable on an open car with normal doors and no special height or thickness of sill, that the body is absolutely rigid, and the steering wheel is shock- and vibration-free.' This they put down to 'good design rather than excessive structural strength, because the kerb weight of the car is only a moderate 16.25cwt.'

The 101-series Giulia Spider of 1963 has a longer wheelbase, quarter-light windows, bigger rear-view mirror and a fake air-intake to accommodate the slightly taller 1600 engine.

THE SPRINT SPECIALE AND SPRINT ZAGATO

In fact, the first of the 101-series cars to appear was the Sprint Speciale (SS), which had an entirely new body shell drawn by Franco Scaglione for Bertone. A feast of swooping curves, its coupé shape was based on the Giulietta floorpan, and it was clearly descended from the BAT aerodynamic styling exercises of 1953–54, as well as the Disco Volante sports racer. The SS was intended for use in competition, and it was in any case a limited edition, with just 1,366 built between 1959 and 1962.

Another celebrated Italian stylist, Elio Zagato, had been re-modelling the Giulietta Sprint as a lightweight competition car known as the SVZ – Sprint Veloce Zagato – since 1956. It was rounder, lower, and featured his trademark double-bubble roofline; perhaps 18 SVZs were made. Then Zagato went a stage further and between 1960 and 1962 produced the rotund, more compact-looking Sprint Zagato SZ with all-aluminium bodywork and trim. In race trim, teams like the Ambrosiana and Sant'Ambroeus squads ran their SZs with engines prepared by tuning experts Virgilio Conrero and Carlo Facetti. High-lift cams,

While the interior of the Giulia Spider was not altered much, this rare right-hand-drive version shows the new glove compartment door, aluminium-spoked steering wheel, and umbrella-handle handbrake lever.

carburettor mods and lightened flywheels produced between 118 and 127bhp at 7,500rpm. In regular trim, the SZ was powered by the 100bhp Veloce-spec. engine, and its minimal weight – 1,700lb (771kg) – gave it such a good power-to-weight ratio that it became the fastest of the Giuliettas. In 1961 a second-series, the SZ2, was also built on the Giulietta floorpan but was supposedly rather more aerodynamic, and featured the Kamm-tail look. This model was fitted with disc brakes at the front instead of the Giulietta's drums, the first Alfa to receive them. Other cars in the SVZ theme were made by Sergio Scaglietti (Ferrari's coachbuilder) and Michelotti. But Giulietta Spiders were far less in evidence in competition. Their steel bodies and open cockpits, with the required strengthening which that implied, rendered them overweight, although they were driven in events like the Liège–Rome–Liège rally. In the States, SCCA racing rules allowed greater modifications to be made, and Alfa's Ohio

dealer Charles Stoddard won the SCCA's National Championship G-Production class in 1959 and 1960 with his Spider Veloce.

101-Series Cars

The 101-series Spider Normale's model number was 101.03 and the Veloce model was 101.07 – (101.04 and 101.25 for the States) – and the revisions were extended to the body shell as well. Most significantly, the wheelbase was extended two inches (50mm), which altered ride characteristics for the better while slowing up the steering reflex, and in practical terms, the cockpit was also two inches longer than the 750-series car. In consequence, the wider door openings meant longer doors, which now had non-opening quarter light windows. It was no longer a roadster, in the sense that the rear edge of the hood was now attached to the rear scuttle panel and turned neatly into the well behind the seats when folded

Alfa Romeo Giulia Spider (1962–5)

Layout	Monocoque construction, Pininfarina-designed and -built two-seater soft-top
Engine	
Type	Four cylinders in line, front-mounted
Block	Cast aluminium with slip-fit cast-iron cylinder liners, Mahle pistons
Head	Cast aluminium, cross-flow, hemispherical chambers
Bore and stroke	78mm x 82mm = 1570cc (3.04 x 3.19in = 97.77cu. in)
Valves	Two per cylinder, inclined overhead valves. Bucket tappets, shim adjustment
Camshafts	Twin overhead, chain driven from the crankshaft
Drive	Rear-wheel drive
Power output	92bhp at 6,200rpm (Veloce: 112bhp at 6,500rpm)
Compression ratio	9.1:1 (Veloce: 9.7:1)
Induction	Single down-draught Solex carburettor (Veloce: two side-draught twin-choke Webers)
Generator	Bosch LJ/GEG200/12/2700R
Regulator	Bosch RS/VA200/12A2
Starter	Bosch AL/EEFo.7/12R11
Distributor	Bosch VJU4BR41MK
Coil	Bosch TK12A3
Spark Plugs	Spica-Lodge 2HLNG (Veloce: Spica-Lodge RL47)
Transmission	
Type	4-speed manual, Porsche-type synchromesh, aluminium split case
Clutch	Single disc with coil-spring pressure plate, divided prop shaft with front Metalastic joint, double universal joint, slip spline, central support bearing; hypoid rear axle
Ratios	5th, 1:0.791; 4th, 1:1.00; 3rd, 1:1.355; 2nd, 1:1.988; 1st, 1:3.304; reverse, 1:3.010. Final drive: 8:41 (Veloce: 9.4:1)
Suspension and Steering	
Front	Independent by coil springs, wishbones and dampers, anti-roll bar
Rear	Live axle, longitudinal radius arms, transverse link, coil springs and dampers
Wheels and tyres	Bolt-on steel 15 x 4.5in rims, 155-15 tyres
Brakes	Front discs, Alfin drums rear

Dimensions			
Wheelbase	7ft 3in (2.250m)	**Production**	
Front track	4ft 2.5in (1.292m)	Produced	1962–5
Rear track	4ft 1in (1.270m)	Quantity	9,250 units in total
Weight	1,951lb (885kg)		(Veloce produced from 1964–5, 1,091 units)

Performance	
Acceleration	0–60mph (0–100km/h): 11.5sec. (Veloce: 10.5sec)
Maximum speed	106.9mph (171.04km/h) (Veloce: 111.8mph (178.88km/h))
Fuel consumption	23mpg (12.3ltr/100km) urban cycle, 28mpg (10.1ltr/100km) touring, 25mpg(11.32ltr/100km) overall

back. One improvement to creature comfort was a better heater, although the so-called umbrella-handle handbrake lever under the dashboard was still a fixture. And externally they differed again in that the rear lights were larger than the 750-series cars' charming little split-oval units.

A total of 12,490 of the 101-series Giulietta Spiders were produced up to 1962, when the new Giulia series arrived. To all intents and purposes the name change simply heralded an increase in capacity from 1300 to 1600cc, plus the adoption of the five-speed gearbox. Mechanical updates to what came to be regarded as a smoother, stronger engine included the adoption of Bosch distributors instead of Lucas and Marelli units, controversially as it turned out, while valve diameter and cam lift were increased.

THE GIULIA ARRIVES

Minor changes to the interior and trim accompanied the new model, but, visually, the Giulia Spider differed from the Giulietta in having a superfluous air scoop on the bonnet, which was necessary to accommodate the half-inch taller 1600cc engine. The chrome strip down the centre of the bonnet that had adorned the Giulietta Spiders was now absent. The Giulia cockpit was a more sophisticated place to be than the Giulietta's. The trio of dials on the instrument panel had better markings, there was an aluminium-spoked steering wheel with horn and headlamp flasher surrounding the boss, and the passenger glove compartment gained a door. Interestingly, the Spider models were cheaper than the Sprints, which is not the case today, when the current GTV coupé is at least £1000 or so cheaper in the UK than the Spider.

Badging on the lower right of the boot lid

identified whether the car was a Normale or a Veloce. The high-performance variant was introduced again in 1965 as a 112bhp version of the Giulia 101-series Spiders, fitted with the 1570cc twin-cam used in the SS and GTZ models. Understandably, they were nowhere near as economical as the Normale version. By now, all models were equipped with disc brakes, but wheels were still a spindly 4.5J x 15 shod with 155/15 tyres.

THE TOURING-BODIED SPIDERS

Contemporary with the Giulietta and Giulia generation of Spiders were the 102-series 2000 four-cylinder and 2600 straight-six Spiders, similarly shaped but larger and with more linear styling by Touring-of-Milan. The Spider model was meant to be a two-plus-two, but the space behind the two front seats was little more than a glorified parcel shelf.

Originally intended as a replacement for the 1900 range, the 102-series opened with the factory-styled 2000 Berlina and Touring's 2000 Spider in 1958, followed in 1960 by the Bertone-styled Sprint Coupé version – the work of the young Giorgetto Giugiaro. They were powered by the four-cylinder iron block of the old 1900 range, but the valve gear was similar to the Giulietta engine's. Gearboxes were common to both ranges. Performance was hardly stimulating, and the 101-series Giulietta was a far more sprightly drive. By 1962, just over 7,000 units of the 2000 Spider had been built, and they were succeeded by the virtually identical 106-series 2600 model. This range also consisted of the Spider, Sprint Coupé and factory-designed Berlina saloon versions. Compared with the 101- and forthcoming 105-series models, they were much rarer, altogether more costly, and because of their more relaxed touring qualities, seemed to belong in the realms of more exalted and sedate carriages like Aston Martins, Alvis or Bristols.

The under-stressed 2600 six-cylinder engine was an extended version of the 2000 mill, now cast in aluminium, with seven bearing crankshaft, twin overhead cams, hemispherical combustion chambers and a sump located towards the rear of the block like the old 1900's. It produced 130bhp at 5,900rpm, and breathed through triple Solex 44 PHH carburettors, using a common manifold to feed all cylinders, and they gained a reputation for burned valves. Optional Weber carbs were considered preferable.

Suspension was by double wishbones, kingpins, coil springs, dampers and anti-roll bar at the front, with longitudinal radius arms, triangular lateral locator, coil springs and dampers supporting a solid rear axle. Although handling was nothing like as lively as the Giulia Spider, the 2600 could boast excellent ride quality and directional stability. Disc brakes were now fitted all round, and although they came with steel wheels as standard, wire-spokes were probably a more appropriate option.

Visually, the 2600 Spider differed from the 2000 in having a full-width bonnet air intake instead of the 2000's twin 'nostrils', and driving lights in place of the sidelights of the earlier car. When a particular 'look' catches on, you find inevitably that models from different manufacturers are ripe for comparison. For instance, the 2600 Spider was very similar in appearance to the Maserati 3500 sports car of 1962, styled by Alfredo Vignale, and which is even rarer than the Alfa, with only 242 cars made. Just 2,255 units of Touring's 2600 Spider were built between 1962 and 1965, although nearly 7,000 Bertone-styled Sprints were produced during the same period, including

*The 2600 Spider was bodied by Touring-of-Milan and was a more
sedate sports car than its Giulietta and Giulia siblings.*

105 special bodied versions by Zagato and 54 Berlinas by OSI.

A HARMONIOUS AFFAIR

The entire Giulietta range had been a lasting success, and by the early 1960s, the Giulietta and Giulia Spiders were everyone's idea of chic, semi-exotic sports cars, ones likely to be seen whizzing around the Côte d'Azur, yet they were still on the attainable side of a Ferrari or Maserati. By 1966, production of Giulietta and Giulia Spiders totalled 27,437, so they could hardly be thought of as a common sight. But they were a hard act for the Duetto to follow.

The name 'Giulia' implies a grown-up 'Giulietta', and in effect this was the case with the Spiders. Use of the rather obvious Giulietta name is said to have originated at the launch of the Alfa 1900 series in 1950, when a Russian prince remarked of the factory engineers and drivers that there were many Romeos present, but no Giulietta. Someone picked up on this, and the appellation was ascribed to the 750-series Sprint coupé introduced in 1954.

The first of the 105-series Giulias had actually been around for four years by the time the Spider version was launched. The Giulia TI Berlina was first seen in 1962 at Monza, and was an entirely new platform that would form the basis for the long-running Giulia series of saloons, coupés and Spiders. The 105-series coupé also beat the new Spider by three years: the Bertone- (or Giugiaro-, if you prefer) styled Giulia Sprint GT came out in 1963. In the meantime, the company continued to build the 101-series Giulia Spiders.

However, the new generation of 105-series Spiders would go on to outlive its siblings. It was in production for 27 years, which is not quite a record when compared

Frontal treatment of the 1964 Giulia Spider is wonderfully flamboyant with bags of chrome trim ladled on. Bonnet scoop gives it a grown-up appearance, backed up by its bigger 1570cc engine.

with long-lived icons like the Morgan, Caterham Seven, Porsche 911, Citroën 2CV, Mini and VW Beetle, but still pretty amazing nevertheless. It took over from the 101-series Giulia, starting with the appearance in 1966 of the Pininfarina-designed Duetto.

In fact, this model grew out of a styling project, the last undertaken by Battista Pininfarina before his death. It drew on elements seen the year previously in the Giulietta Spider Speciale *Aerodynamica* prototype, including features like the sloping, rounded front, plexiglass headlight covers, the deep 'cuttlefish' scallop down the sides, and the boat-tail rear end.

From the rear, the Giulia Spider is just as shapely, with quite narrow shoulders. Prominent are the larger 101-series rear lights, Alfa logo boot catch and 1600 insignia.

When the factory was preparing for the launch at the Geneva show in 1966 – the major motoring event of the year – Alfa Romeo decided to gain a little extra publicity by running an international 'name-the-car' contest, and out of some 140,000 entries, the appellation 'Duetto' was the one which stuck in the end. The lucky winner was one Guidobaldo Trionfi of Brescia. His proposition was that the term 'Duetto' is all-encompassing, implying two seats, two carburettors, two camshafts, and a song for two people in harmony with the world in general.

ON THE SILVER SCREEN

Such a charismatic car as the 105-series Spider was bound to be sought after and is still frequently used as a prop in the filming of adverts. However, its finest hour was probably its starring role alongside Dustin Hoffman and Anne Bancroft in the 1967 movie *The Graduate*, set to the unforgettable Simon and Garfunkel soundtrack. After a few tantalising clips while he dithers around Los Angeles, the film climaxes with Hoffman's epic Duetto drive to the university and on to the church – on foot after running out of petrol – to win back his sweetheart, Katharine Ross.

A later film, which features an earlier car, *The Day of the Jackal* contains much memorable footage of Edward Fox as the suave assassin travelling from Italy to France in a bid to eliminate President de Gaulle, in a 101-series Giulietta Spider. The car is resprayed from white to blue to disguise it, and Fox hides the components of a rifle in the car's silencer.

Thirty- and forty-something film-goers may not have actually realized it was a Duetto when they saw *The Graduate*, but when told that's what Hoffman was driving, everyone can immediately remember it, 'the little red Italian job with the floor shift', as someone put it. Dustin Hoffman's Duetto later found its way to Denver, Colorado, where it earned its living as a race car. In fact, two Spiders were used in the making of the film, and both were pensioned off to Alfa Romeo's Southern California Parts Department. Running in the vivid orange and black house colours, one of them was driven to second place by Lee Midgley in the 1968 SCCA championships. This particular car passed into the care of Dale MacGowan, a Denver Alfa specialist, who raced the car in club events. Although the body shell was original, the

The handsome 2600 Spider of 1962 was built by Touring-of-Milan, and bore strong similarities to Vignale's Maserati 3500 of 1960-62, and indeed Touring's own Maserati offering, the 3500GT. Only 2,255 2600 Spiders were made between 1962 and 1966, compared with around 7,000 of the 2000 Spider which it succeeded, and a similar quantity of the Bertone-designed 2600 Sprint coupé version.

car was dominated by its roll cage, as comprehensive as any fitted on a modern Caterham racer. And with its minimal plastic windshield and sponsor decals, it bore little resemblance to its former incarnation as a film star.

Bizarrely, the most recent appearance of the Spider on the flickering tube that I can recall was in the BBC television sitcom *Absolutely Fabulous*. This episode featured my two favourite heroines Jennifer Saunders and Joanna Lumley behaving in predictably outrageous *Ab-Fab* style, causing anarchy in the West End with one of the last of the classic Spiders. 'Edina', who has been encouraged to give up her limo and chauffeur in an economy drive, ends up being fined £50,000 and banned for life for drunken and careless driving, but, mercifully, she doesn't actually bend the Spider. Unusually, it was finished in that gorgeous *amaranto* maroon that one is always hoping to come across but which is actually so rare to find in this country.

BRAND NEW CLOTHES

The rounded nose of the Duetto, emphasized by the perspex headlight fairings, is slightly higher and more bulbous than the rotund tail when the car is seen in profile; the proportions are superb, with or without the hood erect. Seen from above, its shape is perfectly symmetrical.

In terms of mechanical specification, the Duetto had an easy time of it. All the major technical evolutions had been carried out on the Giulietta and Giulia Spiders, so that the Duetto's specification was fairly well settled. Disc brakes were now fitted all round, and the 1,570cc, five-bearing crank, DOHC engine was carried over from the 101-series car. It was now mated to a five-speed all-synchromesh gearbox. The suspension set up was similar to the older car, although its track now measured 0.8in (20mm) wider at the front. Overall length increased by 1ft 1.9in (353mm) due to the greater overhangs at front and rear, while the Duetto's bulbous sides increased width marginally by 2.2in (56mm). It was slightly lower – by 1.9in (48mm) – than the previous model, but weight was a comparable if slightly heavier 2,195lb (955.7kg). The ZF Gemmer steering box ratio was thought to be on the low side, requiring excessive effort and application of much lock for tight turns. The first Duettos fitted with the Dunlop brakes – including hydro-mechanical rear calipers – were not too good at stopping, but they soon gained the better ATE system fitted on all other 105-series Giulias. However, they still lacked a servo, which

Although the dashboard and controls of the 2600 Spider appear rather confused and unco-ordinated, everything is focussed on the driver. It was a more luxurious affair than the Giulietta Spider, and there was even just about enough room for two people in the back seat.

made for a hard pedal and developed powerful calf muscles, but a retro-fit Girling Power-Stop servo kit was available in the UK.

One would imagine that with its mechanical specification sorted, the Duetto had nothing further to worry about, and should have been free to flaunt its brand new clothes. But following the elegance of its long-running predecessors, the Duetto was not a unanimous hit. *Road and Track* magazine described it as 'a contrived design with meaningless styling gimmicks', and 'Pininfarina missed the ball this time'. Nevertheless, although it shared the same wheelbase dimensions, the long tail provided a fair amount of space (7.5 cu.ft./2.12 cu. m) for a sports car. The boot lid was unlocked and the catch released by a lever recessed in the right-hand door jamb. The spare wheel was housed in a well in the boot floor, and the jack was attached to the forward wall of the boot by a large butterfly nut. As a safety precaution, the wheel nuts

were threaded different ways according to which side of the car the wheel was on, and this proved a source of aggravation when changing wheels following a puncture.

Covering Up

The Duetto's weather protection was considered superior to that of its predecessors'. Putting up or taking down the hood has always been straightforward on classic Alfa Spiders; two clasps, one at either side where the hood meets the windscreen, are flipped up, and, pushing up with the central handle, the hood rises in an arc overhead to fall to rest in its well behind the rear 'passenger' space. If it rains and the top is down, you won't get too wet provided you're going fast enough. Modern generation sports cars are a great deal better than their 1960s counterparts, and so they should be. But the operation of the classic Alfa Spider hood should have been an object

Engine bay of the 2600 Spider, revealing the all-aluminium 2584cc six-cylinder engine and its triple Solex 44 PHH carburettor.

lesson to the majority of convertible manu-facturers, in terms of its simplicity and effectiveness. To erect the hood, which you can just about manage while the traffic lights are at red, you heave the central handle up and over your head and juggle the male and female parts on the hood and the windscreen, and flip the clasps down at either corner. When the hood is up, there is a sizeable area of fabric blocking the rear three-quarter view, and with its black upholstered interior, some people find Spider travel somewhat claustrophobic. In

a 1967 report, *Autocar* deemed the Duetto's most serious fault to be 'excessive wind noise: at speeds above about 70mph in top, wind roar began to drown the engine until at high speeds the engine was barely audible at all. Pulling or pushing at the hood,' they said, 'or altering the positions of the windows made no difference, so the noise would not appear to be due to poor sealing.' They concluded that lowering the hood made some improvement, but weren't all sports cars like that? A factory hard-top was available, but its linear,

Conceived in 1966, the Duetto's name was the result of a competition, drawn from some 140,000 entries. In this context, 'Duetto' implies two seats, two carburettors, two camshafts and a song for two people.

Alfa Romeo Duetto (1966–7)

Layout	Monocoque construction, Pininfarina-designed and -built two-seater soft-top
Engine	
Type	Four cylinders in line, front-mounted
Block	Aluminium with cast-iron cylinder liners
Head	Aluminium
Bore and stroke	78 x 82mm = 1570cc (3.04 x 3.19in = 95.77cu.in)
Valves	Two per cylinder, inclined overhead valves. Sodium-cooled exhasut valves are 31mm diameter, inlets: 37mm diameter, set at 80 degrees in hemispherical combustion chamber
Camshafts	Twin overhead, chain driven from the crankshaft
Drive	Rear-wheel drive
Power output	109bhp at 6,000rpm
Compression ratio	9:1
Induction	Two side-draught twin-choke Webers carburettors
Transmission	
Type	5-speed manual
Clutch	Single dry plate, divided prop shaft, hypoid rear axle
Ratios	Top, 1:0.79; 4th, 1:1.00; 3rd, 1:1.35; 2nd, 1:1.99; 1st, 1:3.30; reverse, 1:1.301. Final drive: 4:56:1
Performance	
Acceleration	0–60mph (0–100km/h): 11.2sec.
Maximum speed	113mph (185km/h)
Fuel consumption	22mpg (12.3ltr/100km) urban cycle, 28mpg (10.1ltr/100km) touring, 25mpg(11.32ltr/100km) overall
Suspension and Steering	
Front	Independent by coil springs, wishbones and dampers, anti-roll bar
Rear	Live axle, lower trailing arms, transverse link, coil springs and dampers
Wheels and tyres	Bolt-on steel 15 x 4.5in rims, 155-15 tyres
Steering	Worm and roller
Brakes	Hydraulically operated discs all round
Dimensions	
Length	14ft 0in (4.250m)
Width	5ft 4in (1.630m)
Height	4ft 3in (1.290m)
Wheelbase	7ft 4in (2.250m)
Front track	4ft 3in (1.292m)
Rear track	4ft 2in (1.270m)
Weight	2,180lb (990kg)
Boot	7.5cu ft
Fuel tank capacity	10gal (45.4ltr)

Production

Produced	1966–7
Quantity	6,325 units in total

The Giulia GTC was basically a Giulia Sprint GT with the top cut off. The work was carried out by Touring, and considerable strengthening of the bulkheads was carried out to maintain its rigidity. 1,000 units were produced between its introduction at Geneva in 1965 and 1967.

angular styling sat a trifle oddly on the curvaceous Duetto.

THE GTC

The GTC was a soft-top with a different flavour. It was a four-seater cabriolet, really following on in the tradition of the 6C-2500 and 1900s of the early 1950s. It was therefore stylistically along very different lines to the Spiders, although it shared the same running gear as the Duetto. It was announced at the 1965 Geneva show, and was basically the Bertone coupé version of the new 105 Giulia series, the Sprint GT, with the top cut off, and the shell suitably stiffened by Touring-of-Milan. The GTC was undoubtedly one of the most stylish cabriolets ever made, but production lasted for only a couple of years, during which time a mere thousand cars were assembled. As with all soft-top cars, water leaking into

the innermost recesses of the body shell was its worst enemy, and survivors are now rare and desirable cars.

CREATURE COMFORTS

Like most of its contemporaries, and even on not-so-old vehicles, night-time driving in the Duetto was not an entirely pleasurable experience. The Carello headlights provided good illumination on high beam, but the transition to dip was disappointing. One solution to this was to plug in rally-standard 100-watt bulbs and bigger fuses if they blew, while it wasn't unheard of to retrofit cars with aircraft landing lights. Certainly one way of improving matters a bit was to say goodbye to aesthetics and dispense with the Spider's natty perspex fairings, which restricted the beam slightly. In any case, these have not been legal in Europe for some time, and never were in the States.

63

From the outset, the Duetto suffered from what lanky northern European types describe as the 'typical Italian Ape' driving position. This is to say that the relationship between the pedals and the steering wheel means that anyone without long arms had to sit uncomfortably close to the black Bakelite wheel, which was of an uncomfortably large diameter in the Duetto, and with legs widely splayed at the knees. The Spiders that followed got the characteristic wood-rimmed wheel with the horn buttons located in the three spokes, and, in its final incarnation, leather-rim wheels were standard fittings.

While the Duetto's PVC upholstered seats would seem inadequate today in almost every respect, they were thought to be quite satisfactory in 1966. They were rather low affairs, and there was a knack of getting into a Duetto, or indeed any Spider. In order to preserve a modicum of dignity in the era of the mini-skirt, if you were female presumably, the technique was to insert the backside first and swing the legs in afterwards. By comparison with other sports cars, the Duetto's cockpit was no more and no less austere, although by later Spider standards it was decidedly plain. The Duetto had a new instrument layout, all dials made by Jaeger in Italy and resplendent with Italian nomenclature like *Dinamo* and *Riscald*. The 8,000rpm tachometer and 140mph (225kph) speedometer placed right in front of the driver in a recessed binnacle-type hood. Auxiliary instruments, fuel, oil pressure and water temperature were angled towards the driver and located in the centre of the painted metal dash. In a *Motor Sport* road test in 1967, editor Bill Boddy found the petrol gauge accurate when the car was stationary, but complained that 'the needle floats when on the move'. He recorded an average fuel consumption of 25.3mph,

(11.2/100km) complaining vociferously about transport minister Barbara Castle and how the wretched 70mph (110kph) limit precluded any legitimate attempt at assessing the car's top speed. While the Duetto owner could venture out in the wet with better protection than his Giulietta-driving predecessor could, the 105-series heater was also an improvement.

THE TUBOLARE ZAGATO

The Duetto was based on the same floorpan and was mechanically virtually identical to the 105-series Giulia TI and Super saloon that preceded it by four years. Together with the Bertone-designed Sprint GT coupé of 1964, they were directly related to the

Being a four-seater with a cabriolet-style body, the Giulia GTC harked back in some ways to the 6C 2500- and 1900-based luxury-market cabriolets of the late 1940s and early 1950s.

Unlike the contemporary Giulia Spider and Duetto, the GTC's weather equipment featured sophistications like wind-up rear three-quarter windows.

GTZ (or TZ 1) racing coupé which first appeared in 1963. This 'Tubolare Zagato' model was intended as a competition car and differed from the rest of the 105-series cars in having a tubular steel frame built up on the Giulia floorpan supporting a curvaceous aluminium low-drag Zagato body. Weighing only 1,430lb (649kg), it had full independent suspension and the 1600 Veloce twin-cam was canted over to the left for improved running, with specially cast sump and manifolds to compensate. As befitted a race car, the interior was suitably spartan with no sound insulation and luggage space was shared with the alloy spare wheel and 25-gallon (113.5-litre) fuel tank. The TZ1s were raced from 1964 to 1965 by the Autodelta team, backed by Carlo Chiti's works, and were superseded by the altogether more aggressive-looking TZ2 from 1965 to 1966. Many class wins were achieved in events like the Le Mans 24 Hours, Nurburgring 1,000kms, Targa Florio and Sebring 12 Hours. Predictably for a competition model, production volumes were minute: just 112 TZ1s and only 11 TZ2s were ever built.

Specifications

At the time, all Giulia models used Alfa Romeo's familiar 1.6-litre in-line four-cylinder twin-cam engine, while the Sprint, Spider and later the Super saloon were fed by twin side-draught Weber carburettors. The water-cooled engine's capacity was 1,570cc, an all-aluminium unit with cast-iron cylinder liners. These barrels were tapered and fitted precisely into the block, forming a 'wet-liner' design that allowed for uniform cooling around each barrel. Coolant was prevented from getting into the sump by thin rubber seals around the base of the barrels.

The cam journals in the cylinder head were lubricated via six small oil channels. The lubricant was fed back to the broad new 105-series cast-aluminium T-shaped sump (sometimes referred to as a 'batwing' or 'hammerhead' shape) through three oval holes at the rear of the block and the timing chain compartment at the front. In the head were the hemispherical combustion chambers with the spark plugs in the top, and the valves opened and closed by means of inverted-cup tappets, operated by chain-driven camshafts. The exhaust valves were sodium-cooled, and the crankshaft had five main bearings. Power output was quoted as 125bhp (SAE), 109bhp (DIN), at 6,000rpm, giving a top speed of 113mph (182kph) and a 0–60mph (0–100kph)-acceleration time of 11.3 seconds. As an interesting aside, at this time Alfa Romeo engines were also popular fitments in hydroplanes and racing powerboats.

Servo-assisted Dunlop disc brakes were fitted all round, and front suspension was independent by double wishbones, coil springs and dampers, and an anti-roll bar. The rear suspension featured a live axle, on coil springs and dampers, located by lower trailing arms and a reaction trunion. The Duetto was shod with 155 x 15 tyres, which were tall and skinny, even by the standards of 1966. In 1967, the improved ATE brakes were fitted, although there was as yet no servo assistance. Cylinder-head porting was also improved at this time.

When new, the Alfa Romeo Duetto cost £1,894.12s.9d in the UK, which made it significantly more expensive than all its rivals bar the Marcos 1600 at £1,860, and the E-type Jaguar at £2,068. The Healey 3000 Mk III was a snip at £1,126, and the Lotus Elan a mere £1,553. Therefore the Duetto appealed to a particular type of sports car buyer, probably someone who appreciated the car's lively performance and handling, but who didn't need the extra power available in the E-type, and found that too big and ostentatious anyway. The Duetto buyer's profile would most likely have been that of a wealthy enthusiast. Its production spanned just two years: 1966 and 1967, during which time 6,320 units were made.

GRAN SPORT QUATTRORUOTE

Pastiches of classic cars are outside the main thrust of the motor industry, and are regarded by many as superficial and irrelevant. And nice as some of them undoubtedly are, I wouldn't be content with anything except the genuine article: a Porsche 911 please, not a Covin copy. The cost factor is clearly the overwhelming motive for people intent on buying a 'replicar'. For better or worse, there is a thriving industry specializing in copies of legendary sports vehicles, from Safir's GT-40s and Lynx's D- and E-types, to Westfield Sevens and a whole nest of 'fake snake' Cobra copies. Some are terrible concoctions: I've even seen an imitation Bugatti Type 35 powered by a VW Beetle engine – mounted in the rear!

'Replicars' are a relatively modern phenomenon, however, brought on by the astronomical price rises of the late-eighties, which took many desirable models out of reach of the average enthusiast. Back in 1965, though, the Italian car magazine *Quattroruote* sponsored an interesting exercise in retro-design when it commissioned Zagato to produce 92 units of a sports car based on the 1929–33 Alfa Romeo 6C-1750 Zagato. Thus it had the classic Gran Sport's authentic-looking clamshell wings with independent headlamps, running-boards, flat radiator, wire-spoke wheels (of smaller diameter) and the spare mounted on its round rump. Chassis and running gear were up to the minute, however. It was done during a time of transition, and although they fitted the stock 105-series Giulia engine with single Solex carb, the suspension and drive train that Zagato used were the leftovers from the 101-series parts bins. The 4R Zagato 'replicars' were sneered at by purists, but

The Gran Sport Quattroruote was a pastiche of the Zagato-bodied 6C-1750 Spider of the late-twenties and early-1930s. It was commissioned from Carrozzeria Zagato in 1965 by the Italian Quattroruote magazine, and 92 were made, using the running gear and suspension of the 101-series Giulia. Its relationship to the proportions of the original car was to an extent spoilt by the smaller 15in (40cm) wheels, but even so, it captured the flavour of vintage motoring pretty well. This is probably the only one in the UK and belongs to Remco and Jill Caspers, pictured at National Alfa Day.

were well-made and swift because of their lightness, as well as being fun to drive.

Other special 105-series Alfas of the late 1960s were the GTA, the lightweight version of the Sprint GT and its smaller capacity sibling, the GTA 1300 Junior. These irrepressible racers made a name for themselves all over the world in touring car racing, while the purpose of the special bodied Junior Zagato of 1969 was less easy to define. Zagato's expertise was clearly evident in the TZ2 racers but paradoxically their Junior Z model was steel-panelled rather than in aluminium. Kamm tails did not come much more prominent than this, and the full-width plexiglass front panel gave the car something of a belligerent appearance. However, its real purpose

was not for competition use, but simply as a more radical road-going coupé than the regular Sprint GT. After 1,108 units had been produced with the 1300cc Giulia engine, the Junior Z was fitted with the 1600cc motor in 1972.

Tax breaks also played a part in company thinking. It was advantageous to bring out the Spider 1300 Junior in 1969, and this model was built in small numbers (totalling less than 3,000 units) until 1972. For similar reasons it is unusual to see cars with engines bigger than 2.0-litres in Italy because it costs more to licence them. When touring in Italy with a 2.5-litre GTV6, I was amazed when an Alfa dealer actually came out of his showroom to admire the car because it was such a rare sight there.

The Duetto was given the 1779cc engine in 1967, and from then onwards was called the 1750 Spider Veloce. Apart from the 1750 identification on the boot-lid, it was externally identical to the Duetto, until it got the Kamm-tail chop in 1969.

THE 1750 SPIDER VELOCE

Along with the 1750 Berlina saloon and the GTV version of the Sprint GT, the 1750 Spider Veloce appeared in 1967. These models were not available in the US until 1969 however, and in typical Alfa style, the old 1600cc Giulia Super saloon continued to be made until 1972. The Berlina contrived to be a slightly larger car than the Giulia Super/TI, with better leg room inside and a more capacious boot. But it lacked the older model's wonderful fluted lines along flanks and roofline, and therefore its quirky character. I ran a 1750 Berlina for a while in the mid-1970s, and the performance and

handling capabilities of such an innocuous-looking car surprised not a few people, including, I recall, the occupants of a Dolomite Sprint in the Lake District. This was the saloon that all the hot-shoes liked to have back then, and these guys were clearly astonished that the Berlina could hold them on a twisty road, even if it lagged a bit on the long straight sections. Even so, the 1750 Berlina was quite at home loping along a motorway-class road at a relaxed 100–110mph (160–177kph).

But back in the tangled web of 1967, the 1750 Spider could lead the opposition a merry dance. Still sporting the Duetto's curvaceous boat- or round-tail body and perspex headlight fairings, the new 1750

Spider was virtually identical to its predecessor, except that it now had 14-inch, instead of 15-inch diameter wheels. Apart from the more or less unnoticeably taller block of the 1779cc engine, the 1750 cockpit featured a dished wood-rim steering wheel, and instruments angled towards the driver. The 1750's only other distinguishing feature was its rear anti-roll bar, a first for production Spiders, and a positive move towards decreasing the characteristic Alfa understeer. John Bolster, writing *Autosport*'s road test report in 1969, said the 1750 Spider Veloce was: 'The kind of car that even an experienced test driver will take out for the sheer fun of handling it. When driven hard, the car is beautifully balanced, understeering at first but tending to oversteer progressively as more power is applied. It feels very well balanced, never doing anything unexpected and responding at once to the merest flick of the wheel.' Putting it through its paces, Bolster said: 'On the road, 120mph is often seen, though the honest, timed maximum is a little below

this. There is no need to engage fifth speed below 100mph or so, but the car is in fact surprisingly flexible on this high gear.' We tend to take all this for granted now, but clearly the 1750 was making a good impression back then. 'The forward weight distribution is noticeable because wheelspin is rather easily induced when getting away,' said Bolster, 'matching a fast upchange, or when accelerating hard out of a slow corner. As is usual with rigid axles, the propeller shaft torque causes the wheel on the right side to spin first, and faster getaways could be made with a limited slip differential.' As we know, Alfa Romeo was already on the case, and the 1750's successor would have the LSD back axle.

SPICA INJECTION

The US-spec cars weighed in at 2,346lb (1,064kg), some 58lb (26kg) heavier than their European counterparts. They were equipped with the much-maligned Spica

The often-maligned Spica mechanical fuel injection system was fitted to all Alfas imported into the USA between 1969 and 1981, and was developed to comply with the emissions control regulations. Although the fuel pump motor brushes wore prematurely, a properly adjusted Spica system provided exactly the same performance as carbs.

Alfa Romeo 1750 Spider Veloce (1967–71)

Layout	Monocoque construction, Pininfarina-designed and -built two-seater soft-top
Engine	
Type	Four cylinders in line, front-mounted
Block	Aluminium with cast-iron cylinder liners
Head	Alumininium
Bore and stroke	80 x 88.5mm = 1779cc (3.12 x 3.45in = 108.52cu.in)
Valves	Two per cylinder, inclined overhead valves.
Camshafts	Twin overhead, chain driven from the crankshaft
Drive	Rear-wheel drive
Power output	65bhp at 6,100rpm (Veloce: 90 bhp at 6,500rpm)
Compression ratio	9.5:1
Power output	118bhp at 5,600rpm
Induction	US spec. cars, Spica mechanical indirect fuel injection; two side-draught twin-choke Weber carburettors
Transmission	
Type	5-speed manual
Clutch	Single dry-plate, divided prop shaft, hypoid rear axle
Ratios	Top, 1:0.79; 4th, 1:1.00; 3rd, 1:1.35; 2nd, 1:1.99; 1st, 1:3.30; reverse, 1:1.301.
	Final drive: European cars: 4.10:1; US cars: 4.56:1
Suspension and Steering	
Front	Independent by coil springs, wishbones and dampers, anti-roll bar
Rear	Live axle, longitudinal radius arms, transverse link, coil springs and dampers
Wheels and tyres	Steel, 14 x 5.5in rims, 165HR-14 tyres
Brakes	Discs all round, with twin servo assistance from 1970
Dimensions	
Wheelbase	7ft 4in (2.250m)
Front track	4ft 3in (1.290m)
Rear track	4ft 2in (1.270m)
Weight	2,180lb (885kg)
Fuel tank capacity	10gal (45.4ltr)
Performance	
Acceleration	0–60mph (0–100km/h): 10.0sec.
Maximum speed	115mph (184km/h)
Fuel consumption	21mpg (13.48ltr/100km) urban cycle, 31mpg (9.13ltr/100km) touring, 26mpg(10.88ltr/100km) overall
Production	
Produced	1967–71
Quantity	4,672 to European spec., 4,050 to US spec: 8,722 units in total

mechanical fuel injection, and identified with an *iniezione* badge on the boot lid. This system was specially developed to address the US Environmental Protection Agency's particular laws to control emissions and fitted to all Alfas imported into the States between 1969 and 1981. The injection pump was sourced from Alfa's diesel Auto-carro (truck) engine, and as well as the US-spec. 1750 and 2000cc engines, it also saw service on the Montreal, GTA Juniors, and even the Autodelta-developed flat-twelve Formula 1 engine. The fuel pump proved to have a short life due to motor brushes wearing prematurely, and inadequate service back-up in the States found owners and unqualified hands tinkering with a system that definitely required professional, by-the-book maintenance. There were just 120 Alfa dealers in the entire USA in 1969, and

thus many despairing US Spider owners swapped their injection systems for a good old twin Weber carb. set up. On the other hand, a properly adjusted Spica system provided exactly the same performance as carburettors, without the question-mark as to whether the engine would start. *Car and Driver* magazine said in October 1969 that: 'Although the fuel injection system has a manually adjustable cold start enrichment valve, the 1750s are reluctant to get down to the job in hand, and until the water temperature reaches its standard 190-degrees [Fahrenheit] operating range, engine response is poor.' However, the writer went on, 'Once warmed up and under way everything falls into place, and you discover that the 1750s are among the easiest cars in the world to drive smoothly.' The very last of the classic Spiders with their Bosch Motronic

By 1968, the Spider and Sprint GT ranges had been extended by inserting engines of different displacement, thereby attracting a wider ownership. This gem, with plexiglass headlight cowls now absent, is the Spider 1300 Junior, powered by the well-proven 1290cc engine.

Luggage space was slightly reduced in the truncated Spider tail, but aerodynamics were said to have benefited. Graphics were relocated onto the rear panel.

injection systems, which we shall come to later, were peerless performers, and in a sense relegated carburettors to the history books.

The 1750 Spider Veloce was available until 1971, and alongside it was marketed the round-tail 1300 Junior. Road testers loved to drive them _Road and Track_ outlined the reason why the Spider was such a charmer on the road: 'By using relatively soft springs and controlling body-lean with anti-roll bars, the designers provided a comfortable, controlled ride and lovely handling.' They also praised the 1750's directional stability: 'As speeds increase, there is a gradual transition from understeer to oversteer. Soft tyre

pressures,' they went on, 'were part of the combination too, so cornering power is not high unless they're raised.' Unofficially, there were in fact two 1750 Giulias, known as the Mark 1 and Mark 2 versions, but with visual differences confined to the Coupé models. The downside of the early 1750 Spider, produced until 1970, was its rough-sounding engine, which was the consequence of high-compression piston slap. Better pistons and camshafts were fitted to alleviate this symptom, and, probably more significantly, a second servo was added to boost the braking power. The most drastic change to the Spider's appearance came in 1971 with the introduction of the square-tail models.

The 1750 Spider Veloce's cockpit featured improved seats with integral head rests, twin-binnacle speedo and rev-counter, and the more sophisticated instruments and console paraphernalia of contemporary Alfa models.

Front license plates always posed something of a problem for the Spider's aesthetics, especially in the UK, and one solution was the stick-on variety, as seen on Simon Goodchild's 1750 Kamm tail car.

THE KAMM TAIL

When Alfa Romeo decided to implement the results of wind tunnel tests in 1971, the 1750 Spider Veloce had its pretty tail chopped off, thus shortening the car by a significant 6.2in (158mm). The majority of motoring publications applauded the new look, which was much more up-to-the-minute. 'Aesthetically, it looks much better than before', said Mel Nichols writing in *Sports Car World* in 1972, although in 1971, *Road and Track* viewed the change with indifference, feeling that: 'We don't consider this change to be much improvement, if any.' The writer also remarked

that: 'The body was designed and built by Pininfarina, from whom we expect – and generally get – better than this.'

Their appraisal was correct, because although Alfa Romeo made all the mechanical components, production of the cars was largely in the hands of Pininfarina. Alfa Romeo Spiders went down the track alongside Fiat 124 Spiders and Fiat Dinos. Before total manufacture passed over to Pininfarina, completed and trimmed body shells were transported to Arese to have the drive trains installed. There was no robotization in the assembly procedure because the car was designed before such techniques came into being. The later cars came to be finished in two-pack acrylic instead of cellulose, and the factory assured me that the Spider's anti-corrosion treatment was regularly updated. Read Chapter 5 on Restoration to see how effective it was.

At the same time as the introduction of the Kamm tail (named after Prof. Wunibald Kamm, who demonstrated in the early fifties that a sharply truncated body is endowed with a markedly improved drag coefficient), a few other alterations were made, including the slight lowering and widening of the grille aperture, recessing the door handles, and restyling the bumpers with rubber facings. The windscreen was given a bit more rake, and the floorpan pressings were altered, with the effect that leg room was marginally reduced. With the removal of several inches from the back end of the car, there was not surprisingly also a slight loss in luggage-carrying capacity – from 7.5cu.ft. to 6.9cu.ft (2.1cu.m. to 1.95cu.m.).

For the most part, Spiders have left the racing side of things to their coupé cousins. In the USA, however, the more liberal rules enabled owners to modify their Spiders to greater effect, like this Giulietta 'Sebring' belonging to Franco Burdisso and Claudio Ladisa. It awaits scrutineering at the Zagarella Hotel prior to the Targa Florio retrospective of 1986. Behind it is a Fiat Ermini 1100 Sport and, at left, an Alfa 1300 SS.

Zagato's Junior Z model was panelled in steel rather than aluminium, featuring a prominent Kamm tail and a full-width plexiglass front panel. It was not destined for competition use, but was a more radical road-going coupé than the regular Sprint GT.

The instrument panel was modified, retaining the binnacle concept, but the hoods shrouding the speedo and rev counter were enlarged. The auxiliary instruments were shifted upwards, and the wood veneer panelling abandoned in favour of black vinyl. Ventilation was improved, with central ducts on top of the dashboard and directional vents at each end of it. The fit and sealing of the hood were also better. What was not improved was the driving position, which many tall drivers still found irksome. There never was any scope for reach adjustment in the steering column. As an aggrieved *Road and Track* reporter put it: 'For those of us with normal arms and legs, shoving the seat back far enough to un-kink the legs puts the steering wheel out of reach unless the seatback is cranked up to full vertical.' The Giulia GTV Coupé and 1750 Berlina were never quite as uncomfortable in this respect as the Spider. Other gripes were mostly of an ergonomic nature, since it was felt that the 1750 Spider was too expensive a car – at £2,199 or $4,800 – to allow for its shortfalls in the comfort zone. They included the lack of an armrest, an awkwardly high accelerator pedal, and the hopeless gesture towards a couple of child seats in the rear. Clothes could be snagged on the window frames, a seat-belt slot was too close to the handbrake, and the positioning of the wiper switch in amongst a trio on the console was potentially dangerous. This location of switchgear made it possible for the unfamiliar driver to turn off the instrument lights by mistake while groping for the wipers. In summary, it appeared that insufficient thought had been paid to the practicalities of living with the car.

As for its seductive appearance, the round tail and low-slung nose of the 1750 were most attractive stylistically, but were hopelessly vulnerable in parking situations,

Alfa Romeo 2000 Spider Veloce and Spider 2.0 (1971–94)

Layout	Monocoque construction, Pininfarina-designed and -built two-seater soft-top
Engine	
Type	Four cylinders in line, front-mounted
Block	Aluminium with cast-iron cylinder liners
Head	Alumininium
Bore and stroke	88 x 88.5mm = 1962cc (3.43 x 3.45in = 119.68cu.in)
Exhaust	Catalytic converter fitted to US cars from 1975, to European cars from 1990
Valves	Two per cylinder, inclined overhead valves
Camshafts	Twin overhead, chain driven from the crankshaft
Drive	Rear-wheel drive
Compression ratio	9.5:1
Power output	132bhp at 5,500rpm (Veloce: 90 bhp at 6,500rpm)
Induction	US spec. cars: Spica mechanical indirect fuel injection. Two side-draught twin-choke Weber carburettors. Bosch fuel injection on European cars from 1990
Transmission	
Type	5-speed manual
Clutch	Single dry-plate, divided prop shaft, hypoid rear axle
Ratios	Top, 1:0.79; 4th, 1:1.00; 3rd, 1:1.35; 2nd, 1:1.99; 1st, 1:3.30; reverse, 1:1.3.01. Final drive: European cars: 4.10:1; US cars: 4.56:1. 25% limited slip differential fitted
Wheels and tyres	Optional alloy 14 x 5in rims, 185 HR x 14 tyres. From 1988, alloy 15 x 6in wheels and 195/60-R15 tyres optional, and standard from 1990
Dimensions	
Length	13ft 6in until 1983, then 14ft 0in (4.250m) (US bumpers from 1975)
Width	5ft 4in (1.630m)
Height	4ft 3in (1.290m)
Wheelbase	7ft 4in (2.250m)
Front track	4ft 4in (1.324m)
Rear track	4ft 2in (1.270m)
Weight	2,288lb (1,040kg)
Boot	7.5cu ft (2.12cu in)
Fuel tank capacity	12gal (54.6ltr)
Performance	
Acceleration	0–60mph (0–100km/h), 8.8sec.
Maximum speed	118mph (188km/h)
Fuel consumption	26mpg (10.88ltr/100km) urban cycle, 36mpg (7.86ltr/100km) touring, 30mpg(9.43ltr/100km) overall
Production	
Produced	1971–94
Quantity	98,643 units in total

although when the Kamm tail was introduced, at least one end of the Spider's body was spared the abuse of the careless parker. That said, the Kamm tail surely unbalances the beautifully rounded matching front and rear ends of the boat-tail car, and there is a strong school of thought which believes that the wonderful free-revving qualities of the 1750 engine make the boat tail the most desirable of the 105-series Spiders.

The Giulietta SZ2 – the long-tailed Sprint Zagato – of 1962, and the TZ1 Tubolare Zagato of 1963 show off the chopped-tail characteristic to excellent effect. However, it is questionable whether the Spider derives any significant aerodynamic benefit from having the operation. It was more likely a plausible justification for updating the appearance, and it was presumably less costly to produce than the round-tail pressings.

One problem that the Kamm tail does throw up is that the back pressure it generates tends to force exhaust gasses back inside the car with unwholesome effects. This was just as true of the later Alfetta GTV models as it was of the square-tail Spider, and could be combated only by such expedients as ensuring that the rubber seals of boot lid or rear hatch were intact, and blanking off rear-light and number-plate fixings inside the boot.

Perhaps the Spider's worst blemish is to

This 1979 US-spec 2000 model shows several of the external indignities the Spider was forced to endure in the interests of environmental protection. Bumpers are like battering rams fore and aft, the suspension has been raised to lift headlight height, and big side indicators disfigure the front and rear wings. Whether the alloy disc wheels suit the car is another matter.

be found at the other end, on its elegant nose, at least in the UK, where the wretched British number plate is so large and prominent as to be completely incongruous. Some drivers fit more unobtrusive motorcycle plates, which are similar in size to the home-market Italian jobs, although I have been advised by the police here that they are illegal. Some people settle for stick-on number plates of conventional UK size across the front panel, and these don't spoil the line of the car, but again, there is a legal argument that these are not clearly visible because they are not at right angles to the road.

UPPING THE CAPACITY

As we have seen, there have been Veloce high-performance options throughout the various model ranges, from the Giulietta

This was the sort of stunt the trade got up to back in 1970, although in this case not quite as risqué as TVR's notorious nude models scam. Paint re-finishing company Valroc used a treated Spider 1300 Junior to publicise its acrylic paint system. Apparently you won a shirt off one of the girls if you could guess the car's mileage....

Interior of the US model shows off leather seats and dished wood-rim wheel.

Spider Veloce, which boasted nearly 40% more power than its sibling, through the various GT Veloces, to the Twin Spark- and 3.0-litre Alfa 75 Veloce of the late-eighties. The latter had no performance modifications, and benefited only in the aesthetics department by having a factory race-replica body kit which I know from personal experience to be a shoddy fitment indeed. As a general rule though, Alfa Romeo has followed the well-worn wisdom of increasing performance in a particular model by upping the engine capacity, and, as we have seen, all four twin-cam variants, from 1300cc to 2.0-litres have found their way at some time into the Spider. Next step after the Duetto then, was to swap the 1600cc unit for the 1750cc engine, thereby

creating a new model and a Veloce version of the Spider concept in one go.

Many owners of later 105-series Alfas have upgraded their car's performance by the simple expedient of dropping in a larger capacity version of the Alfa twin-cam. I progressed from 1300 through 1600 up to 2.0-litres with my Giulia TI, installing a limited slip differential from a 2000 Berlina in the process. It was not quite such a simple operation with the earlier 750-series models, however, although clever engine-swappers have been able to install a 1600 or 1750cc unit without having to alter the bonnet, by playing with the engine-mounting points. One might think that the brakes of a car originally intended to run a 1300cc engine would not be up to the job of slowing

The 2000 Spider Veloce was introduced in June 1971, and was to all intents and purposes the 1750 car with the 1962cc, 132bhp motor fitted. The mechanical specification was upgraded to include a limited slip differential, while the instrumentation was altered so that the auxiliary gauges were inserted between the speedo and rev counter in a cluster of four.

its progress once endowed with 2.0 litres, but the single servo system coped admirably.

SPIDERS IN COMPETITION

Apart from forays into rallies in the mid- to late-1960s, the Spider was never really used as a serious race or rally car. At the level of competition you might expect to find a Spider, the works-backed Autodelta weapon was the GTA, as, clearly, coupé and saloon bodyshells are a lot stiffer than those of regular sports cars. However, Giulietta and Giulia Spiders in radically modified trim were campaigned during this period in the USA in the SCCA championship. Among the class winners in 1600 and 1750 Spiders here were Messrs Bagby, Blizzard, Colman, Griffith, Juckette, Lyon, Locario, Pickett, Rinde, Taggart, Tuttle, Spruell, MacGowan, Midgley and Ward. This clearly indicates that there were a fair number of Giulietta, Giulia and 105-series Spiders in active participation in the USA from the late-1960s to the mid-1970s.

Digging through my copies of Alfa's official results diaries – *Alfa Vince* and *Alfa Corse* – kindly donated by Elvira Ruocco at *Centro di Documentazione Storica Alfa Romeo*, I came across several references to class-winning Duettos, but successes in the main went to GTAs, and not just in Touring Car events, with a smattering of TZs, Tipo 33s and Giulia TI/Supers mentioned, rather than Spiders. But to give you a few examples, Raffi's Spider 1600 won the Gran Turismo 1600 class in a round of the 1967 Italian hill-climb championship. Then a Duetto won the 1600 GT class in the Circuito del Mugello, Tuscany, in 1968, driven by Cecchini/Ans. Luigi Cecchini also won his class in the Siracusa 3 Hours. In 1969 the Beckers/ Stalpaert Belgian Duetto won the GT class in the 12 Hours of Ostend. Christine Beckers was a quasi-works Alfa driver, equally at home behind the wheel of a supercharged GT SA or GTA 1300 J, and she was second overall in the 1969 Tulip Rally in a 1750 Spider Veloce. Another Duetto driven by Reitz/Kober won the GT category of the Deutschland Rallye, while

Racewear specialist Ian Jacobs raced a 2000 Spider in the mid-1980s, before passing the car on to Colin Burnes, who was perhaps slightly less exuberant with it.

With soft-top billowing, the Giulietta Spider of Jack Hamilton leans around Silverstone's Woodcote corner on the old Club circuit in 1961.

Meyer/Dutz took the 1300 class in the ADAC Tour of Europe with a Spider 1300 Junior. Then in 1970 a Group 3 spec 1750 Spider Veloce won its class in the French International Rally, driven by Vion. The records show a number of Duetto successes in minor Italian national rallies in the mid- to late-1960s, with Cecchini and Rossi being the names which crop up most often. They were always in the 1600 GT class, but these were the only Spider victories in a sea of Tipo 33s, TZs and GTA variants.

Classic racing Alfa specialist Julius Thurgood once told me that Autodelta entered a couple of Spiders in the Targa

Florio in the late-sixties, equipped with the GTA's sliding block rear suspension and the 1300 eight-plug head, possibly in response to Fiat's entering a pair of Dinos. I cannot confirm any of this, as 'DSJ' makes no reference in the relevant reports in *Motor Sport*. He mentions Fiat 124 Spiders and the Lancia Fulvia roadsters with their tops cut off, so I imagine he would not have missed any Alfa Spiders that had been so radically modified. However, *Alfa Corse* results sheets mention Capra/Sala winning the 1600 Gran Turismo class in a Duetto in 1968 – the year Alfa were second, third and fourth with Tipo 33s – so maybe this

Alfa Romeo Spider 1300 Junior (1968–72)

Layout	Monocoque construction, Pininfarina-designed and -built two-seater soft-top
Engine	
Type	Four cylinders in line, front-mounted
Block	Aluminium with cast-iron cylinder liners
Head	Alumininium
Bore and stroke	74 x 75mm = 1290cc (2.89 x 2.93in = 78.69cu.in)
Valves	Two per cylinder, inclined overhead, sodium-cooled, set at 80 degrees in hemispherical combustion chamber. Inlet valves 33mm (1.29in), exhaust valves 28mm (1.09in)
Camshafts	Twin overhead, chain driven from the crankshaft
Drive	Rear-wheel drive
Power output	89bhp at 6,000rpm
Compression ratio	9.5:1
Induction	Two side-draught twin-choke Weber carburettors
Transmission	
Type	5-speed manual
Clutch	Single dry-plate, divided prop shaft, hypoid rear axle
Ratios	Top, 1:0.79; 4th, 1:1.00; 3rd, 1:1.35; 2nd, 1:1.99; 1st, 1:3.30; reverse, 1:1.301. Final drive: 4.10:1
Dimensions	
Length	14ft 0in (4.250m)
Width	5ft 4in (1.630m)
Height	4ft 3in (1.290m)
Wheelbase	7ft 4in (2.250m)
Front track	4ft 3in (1.310m)
Rear track	4ft 2in (1.270m)
Weight	2,180lb (990kg)
Boot	7.5cu ft (2.12cu m)
Fuel tank capacity	10gal (45.4ltr)
Kamm-tail bodies from 1970. Hence:	
Length	13ft 6in(4.120m)
Front track	4ft 4in (1.324m)
Rear track	4ft 2.5in (1.274m)
Weight	2,288lb
Fuel tank capacity	12gal (54.6ltr)
Performance	
Acceleration	0–60mph (0–100km/h): 11.4sec.
Maximum speed	98mph (156.8km/h)
Fuel consumption	24mpg (11.79ltr/100km) urban cycle, 30mpg (9.43ltr/100km) touring, 27mpg(10.48ltr/100km) overall

Production

Produced 1968–72

Quantity 4,538 units, plus 249 in 1977–8 = 4,787 in total

Duetto was one of the Autodelta-prepared Spiders. Since there were usually eighty-plus cars entered in this event, from TZs to Sprites, it is not an easy one to research.

Coming more up to date, race-wear specialist Ian Jacobs raced a Spider with considerable aplomb in the UK Alfa Romeo Owners' Club series in the mid-eighties, and the car subsequently reappeared, resprayed, in the hands of Colin Burns. Also memorably, the round tail 1750 Spider of Anthony Ross featured in Alfa Club races in the early 1990s.

Torque Talk

Soon after the advent of the Kamm tail came the capacity increase to the torquier 2.0-litre engine, and the free-revving smaller capacity engines were dropped on the UK market, although the 1750 was still available through the 1971-model year. Alongside the Spiders came the 2000 GTV Coupé and the 2000 Berlina, which for the most part differed externally from their predecessors in grille and badge detail only. The Coupé's grille became a one-piece stylized version incorporating the Alfa 'shield', and was perhaps not the happiest solution. Instrument panels were revised, and interior trim was improved and upgraded with potentially more durable cloth seats. Visually, there is nothing to distinguish the external appearance of the 2.0-litre Spiders from their square-tailed 1750 brethren, apart from the 2000 badge on the back panel. The days of the beautiful *cloisonné* Alfa badge had ended back in 1960, when the Alfa emblem started to be made of plastic.

All the different engine sizes could be obtained on the Spider's home market. In Italy the 1750cc and 1300cc models were phased out in 1971 with the introduction of the 2000 model, but there were invariably overlaps and reintroductions, such as when a number of 1600-engined cars were imported into the UK in the mid-1980s. European cars could be delivered with twin

Anthony Ross racing his immaculate 1750 Spider in an AROC round at sunny Snetterton in 1991. The hardtop improved aerodynamics.

As early as 1974, Pininfarina was showing the Spider Aerodinamico, featuring wide-rim wheels, an aerofoil apron around the lower front panel, and a 'gurney' spoiler on the trailing edge of the boot lid. These modifications were straight off the race circuit, and the car almost looked eligible for SCCA events.

Webers, Dell'Ortos or even Solex carburettors. The first two makes were reckoned to be the best choice. In the States, the 2000cc models were designated 115-series cars, and first appeared there in 1973. As before, they ran with Spica fuel injection.

It was felt that the classic Spider's lines were in need of a face-lift by the mid-1970s, but the benefits of customising like this are debatable.

The increase in capacity was achieved by increasing the 1750 engine's 80mm (3.12in) bore to 84mm (3.28in), and retaining the 88.5mm (3.45in) stroke. There were improvements to the internals, including nitriding the crank to promote less surface wear and thus a longer life, and the intake valves were enlarged for better engine breathing. The camshafts were reprofiled and were now milder than those of the 1750 engine, while the 2000's oil filter was of the screw-in type. A further improvement was that there was no need to adjust the hydraulic clutch slave cylinder, which had been periodically necessary before.

With their increased torque, the 2.0-litre cars could pull more efficiently at low revs,

ultimately developing around 130bhp at 4,500rpm. They could make good use of the power too, thanks to the adoption of a limited slip differential. This enabled them to get more traction out of a slow bend, and helped adhesion on a slippery surface. The cars now also had bigger brakes, although the brakes even on the single-servo 1300cc Giulias were powerful enough to retard the progress of a 2000cc Alfa, as I can confirm from my engine-swapping days.

There were major problems waiting in the wings, however. It soon filtered through the Alfa grapevine that owners of 2000cc cars were complaining more frequently of blown head gaskets. Which, at the risk of becoming tedious, I can endorse too, having

With the demise of the 1750 model, a 103bhp 1600 variant became available once more and was marketed alongside the 2000 Spider Veloce. Apart from changes to satisfy US legislation, the Spider was fundamentally unchanged until 1980. At this point, the dashboard reverted to something more like its 1750 layout while rather surprisingly, according to the catalogue, ball-joint or rack-and-pinion steering could be specified. Hubcaps had been dispensed with in favour of chromed dust caps, although headlight covers were retained.

had at least two let go in spectacular fashion when really 'going for it' in the Giulia TI and an Alfetta GTV. Perversely, the blown head gasket is most easily explained by temperature factors when the engine has yet to warm up. It may be down to the expansion differential of the taller alloy block and cast-iron cylinder liners: when cold, the block shrinks away from the head, which sticks to the tops of the cylinder liners. Under pressure, the oil is then able to force its way past the six O-ring seals betwixt head and block to the detriment of the head gasket.

Replacement usually involves getting the head skimmed as well, and is therefore never going to be a cheap repair.

As we shall see in Chapter 5, the 2000 Spider had a built-in corrosion potential. As well as carpeting, the floorpan had heavy-duty heat- and soundproofing glued onto it, and if the rain got in, it soaked it up and provided a medium for rust to get working on the metal. Since leaks were an inevitable part of sports car ownership, it was debatable which was the worse scenario: to remove the padding altogether and enjoy the already intrusive transmission din even

Right: *The traditional Pininfarina 'f' logo graced the flanks of the classic Spiders until the final facelift in 1989, from which point onward the stylist's celebrated emblem was barely legible on the cars.*

Below: *Chromed door mounted rear-view mirrors were delicately fashioned, with the conical back hinting at an aerodynamic purpose.*

One variation on the Spider theme was this Alfetta-based design exercise shown at the Turin Salon in 1972. It used the 1800 twin cam engine, and the glazing of the Targa-top could be switched from opaque to transparent.

more, or stay mollycoddled and risk the onset of corrosion.

By the mid-1970s, California-spec Spiders were equipped with catalytic converters, having first had to endure the indignity of an air pump mounted incongruously on the front of the engine. The Spider was getting on for ten years old when it was hit by the Federal safety regulations, and clearly these appendages were an afterthought. When the Alfetta models replaced the 105/115-series GTV and Berlina, the Spider carried on going, and it inherited the Alfetta's Bosch roller-type fuel pump. The Spica version was ditched, which was probably a bonus, whereas the new four-into-one exhaust manifold that superseded the original four-into-two version probably was not.

By 1978, all US-spec cars were catalysed, and not just those destined for the West Coast. This was of some consolation to Spider owners Stateside, because this uniformity allowed the manufacturer to recalibrate its engines to perform correctly with catalytic converters, and they proved to be much better than those fitted with just the air pump.

In 1975 a stylistic setback occurred in the fortunes of cars destined for the States. The twin front bumpers on either side of the Alfa shield grille were turned into a projecting one-piece moulded wrap-around affair, with the Alfa grille lost behind it. At the same time, the back bumper assumed the appearance of a rubber-clad reinforced steel joist. This was probably the most retrograde visual downturn the Spider was to suffer, even if it was aimed at compliance with safety legislation.

In order to boost sales towards the end of the decade, US fans could buy 'fully loaded' Spiders endorsed by Niki Lauda and Mario Andretti. There were no performance increments, although a rear 'gurney' spoiler suggested otherwise. Leather upholstery

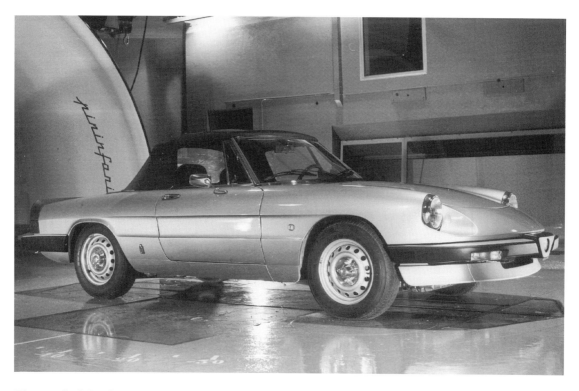

The new look Spider was first seen at the Geneva Show in 1983, incorporating restyled bumpers, front apron and rear 'gurney' spoiler.

was provided, as well as carpeting and air conditioning – in a sports car, whatever next! The Spider's principal market had always been the USA, so the cosseting had to be up to scratch.

Class of '85 college students could even persuade their folks to buy them the 'Graduate' model, which sought to capitalize on the Dustin Hoffman legend. In spite of its basic specification, it got good grades over there, by all accounts.

The 2000 model and its cosmetic permutations were not alone. In 1977 a small number of 1600 and 1300 Spiders were produced – just 248 of the 1300 and 300 of the 1600, in fact, but in 1978 only a single 1300 was made, along with 567 with the 1600 engine. This modest quantity compares with the 3,350 units produced with the 2000 engine in 1978. This rather haphazard arrangement continued through the next decade and reflected a mixture of world-wide market forces, personal tastes and tax advantages.

As its siblings in the Alfa stable kept pace with the changing automotive times of the early 1980s, the Spider grew up, gaining a host of mechanical enhancements. One of these refinements included a compact variable cam-timing device, mounted as part of the drive sprocket on the intake cam. Basically a low-speed emissions enhancement which brought the added benefit of a broader torque band, the vari-cam timer functioned by utilizing the oil pressure to advance the intake cam at higher engine speed, by means of a centrifugal valve. The cam-cover was modified to match.

Spider specifications improved dramatically, particularly in cars for the US market, and in came the Alfetta's variable valve timing, an electronic ignition system triggered by the flywheel, and, most importantly, the GTV6 model's Bosch L-Jetronic fuel injection was incorporated. Electronics now determined the distributor curve, and a sensor was present on the flywheel to eliminate distributor-drive-induced fluctuations in the ignition. The old Spica mechanical fuel injection and the air pump were at last confined to the history books, as the electronic system was not only faster and more accurate in response to throttle demands, it was also infinitely more reliable.

Along with the mechanical updating, the car's structure was also looked at. Sports cars have always suffered from scuttle shake, and in 1982 the Spider body shell was stiffened around the front bulkhead in a bid to minimize this vibration. The move towards a more sophisticated car saw the options list extended to include electric windows.

Over the years, road wheel styles changed four times. The original 105-series steel wheels, with the characteristic air holes running around the outside of the central hub section, had chrome hub caps on the Duetto and 1750 Spiders, losing these in preference for simpler chrome dust-

Overall, the basic 2000 Spider was a tidy package, like this 1984 model fitted with the optional Campagnolo star-pattern alloys. Panel fit was poor in the bumper and rear panel department though, and the all-black rear-end treatment was not a visual success. And the badge graphics looked cheap.

The console was revised yet again, and as brightwork became unfashionable, there was much more matt-black around. Wheel rim and gear knob remained staunchly wooden.

caps with the 2000 Spider. By 1978, customers could specify the finned Campagnolo alloys of the Alfetta 116-series cars. An alternative late 1970s wheel was the flat dish alloy, which looked a bit like a GTV6 wheel and, inevitably, as there is no easier way of customizing your car, other after-market alloys like Cromodora and Momo were sometimes fitted. Although there is one photograph in this book of a Giulietta Spider with wire-spoke wheels, I can only recall ever seeing one or two 105-series Spiders fitted with wire-spoke wheels. They were occasionally applied to the Touring 2600 model, which suited the design. By the time of the Quadrifoglio model, another 'telephone-dial' alloy was available, and this passed on to the last of the 'classic' Spiders, the facelifted car of 1990.

Alfa Romeo UK stopped importing Spiders in 1978, and, as we shall see in another chapter, it was left mainly to specialists Bell and Colvill to import cars into Britain from mainland Europe and convert them to right-hand drive. In 1982 the factory offered two models. There was the regular 2000 Spider Veloce, which carried the full specification, and they also produced a much more basic version, which lacked the frills that the normal car had gathered around it. Since a mere 400 units of these austere Spiders were made, we can assume that Alfa was simply testing the market. Unlike Porsche's 911 Club Sport, where less costs more, this 'Enthusiast's' Spider undercut the Veloce model by nearly £1,000 ($1500).

The US-spec cars became fairly common in Britain following the Spider boom of 1988-9, and UK specialists were left wondering what to make of the North American modifications. Meanwhile, back in 1983, British enthusiasts regarded the latest offerings at Bell and Colvill with amazement.

VARIATIONS ON A THEME

As long ago as the early 1970s, motoring journalists and enthusiasts had been speculating about a replacement for the

The styling department brought the Spider right up to date in 1986 by fitting the Quadrifoglio model with side-skirts and front and rear air dams, complemented by the telephone-dial alloy wheels.

Spider. In 1972 Pininfarina showed an Alfetta-based Targa-top prototype wedge at the Turin Salon, powered by the 1,779cc Alfetta engine, and this gave reason to suppose that Alfa Romeo might be planning a replacement Spider. It featured slim rectangular headlights in a black nose cone, and its simple post-modern interior was set off by the variable glazing of the Targa roof, which could be either smoked or clear. Another Alfetta-based model with slightly more dramatic styling was Pininfarina's Eagle prototype of 1975, which also utilized the Alfetta 1800 running gear. A dramatic aerofoil also acted as the rear support for the Targa roof. The interior was altogether more futuristic in concept with digital instrumentation and velour trim. The

Eagle was probably just too extreme to make it to production, and it was destined to become a resident in the museum at Arese.

Other more recent forays into Spider adaptations on an Alfetta theme have been Simon Hilton's Milano V6 and Sportiva projects of the late 1980s, and the Alfa twin-cam engined Squire also qualifies, although it was another vintage pastiche. The 1991 Minari was again a Spider kit-car project, based this time on Alfasud mechanicals. Pininfarina's own contribution to modern Spider styling came alive most vividly at the 1986 Geneva Salon with a V6-engined Spider remarkably similar to the latest production Spider. There was a GTV-type coupé on show as well. The motoring press thrives on rumour, and coming more up to date, in August 1997, *Autocar* ran a story about a competition version of the current Spider, called the SS. It managed to progress beyond the renderings stage – it was drawn by Centro Stile engineer Filippo Perini – and has been seen at Arese as a show car. Its main features are the roll-over cage around the single-seater cockpit with its fixed tonneau cover, the mandatory air dam and splitter up front, and massive Supertouring alloy wheels. Whether the SS will ever be offered for sale as a 'gentle-man's racer' remains to be seen, but since competition-styled versions of the 156 certainly will be, it should not be ruled out.

CHIN SPOILERS AND FACELIFTS

The facelift that took place in 1983 endowed the Spider with restyled bumpers and an integral Alfa grille, together with a chin-spoiler under the front valance, and a rubber spoiler which extended across the

The final incarnation of the classic Spider was produced in 1990 when it was launched at the Geneva Salon. The body kit of the Quadrifoglio became more integrated with the overall shape of the car, and the nose and tail were much more rounded. Although the standard issue soft-top was of above average quality, the stylish works hard-top fitted on this 1991 Spider as an optional extra made it a really snug and practical car for winter driving.

In 1965 the Italian specialist motoring magazine Quattroruote commissioned Carrozzeria Zagato to recreate its 6C-1750 Gran Sport model from the early 1930s, based on contemporary 101-series Giulia components. Between 1965 and 1968, Zagato built 92 units of the 4R Quattroruote Gran Sport.

One of three Pininfarina pre-production prototype Giulietta Spiders, made in 1955. The design is settled by now, but this version has quarter-light windows that supplement the curvature of the windscreen, and framed sliding side screens.

This immaculate Giulietta Spider Veloce is a 101-series model, because although it lacks the side indicator lenses in the front wings, the chrome strip around the rear of the cockpit and the larger inside rear view mirror date it to 1962. Wind-up windows were introduced in 1959.

(Left) Right-hand drive cockpit and dashboard of the Duetto is a model of simplicity, with Bakelite rim steering wheel and Jaeger instruments. The needles rest at 10mph and 500rpm.

(Below) The straight-six engined Touring Superleggera 2600 Spider was a bigger, more relaxed sports car than the Giulietta, and it replaced the four-cylinder 2000 Touring model in 1962.

The 1750 Spider Veloce like this 1969 model retained the rounded boat-tail of the Duetto, and is reckoned by many purists to be the most desirable of the 105-Series Spiders. It was produced in this format from 1967 to 1971, when the Kamm-tail rear end treatment appeared. All 1750s had dual brake servos fitted and US models got Spica fuel injection from 1969.

While several of the leading carrozzerie experimented with futuristic styling exercises in the mid-1950s, Ghia aimed straight at the US market, which its commercial director Luigi Segre perceived to be most lucrative. This is the Ghia-bodied 1900 Super Sprint Spider of 1955, which was calculated to impress in the States.

Plexiglass headlight cowls were a design feature on all classic 105-series Spiders, including the Duetto and up to the 1983 facelift, although they were absent on the 1300 Junior. They did not enhance illumination potential.

Timeless: from the introduction of the square-tail body onwards, this was the door handle fitted to all classic Spiders.

The Spider's hood was always a good-looking affair, and easy to put up when conditions demanded. New soft-tops are available from upholstery specialists T.A. & J.M. Coburn of Blunsdon, Swindon, Wiltshire. The 2000 Spider Veloce body incorporated a channel around the lower edge of the soft-top, which incorporated four hoses draining water down into the sills. It is vital to ensure that they do not become blocked. The after-market alloy wheels on this 1977 Spider are by Momo.

Rear panel of the 2000 Spider Veloce was relatively uncluttered in the mid-1970s. Alfa Romeo script was to the right, with 2000 identification to the left.

At Pininfarina's plant at Grugliasco, Turin, a US-spec. model with one-piece front bumper heads a line of trimmed and painted Spider bodyshells. This 'safety feature' disfigured all US-market Spiders from 1975 onwards. From Grugliasco, the cars were despatched to Arese to have drive train and running gear installed. To the right is another Pininfarina commission, a line of Peugeot 504 Coupés.

Spider styling was dragged screaming up to date in 1986 with the body-kitted 2.0-litre Quadrifoglio model. It came with electric windows, redesigned seats, instrument panel and revised relationship of pedals, steering wheel and seat. A newly styled removable hard-top was also available for the Quadrifoglio, which suited it rather well.

The rear quarters of the late-model Spider revealed a design which had finally matured. Instead of add-on spoiler and tacky badging, the tail once again assumed the elegant proportions of the Duetto, complete with 164-style rear-light clusters.

(Below) By 1990 the plastic body-kit of the mid-'80s Quadrifoglio model had been so well integrated with the Spider's original architecture that it could be mistaken for a new model. After driving models representing a cross-section of all the Spiders, Tipler decided that if the funds were available, this was the evolution that he would go for – and that included the latest model.

*New meets old: the
1990 Spider looks at
home beside the most
venerable Italianate
architecture.*

*In 1990 the Spider
went through its
final metamorpho-
sis in its classic
guise. The bodykit
that had trans-
formed the Quadri-
foglio had now
merged into the
overall styling
package.*

The Spider hit the bright lights in 1995, and took front of stage on Alfa Romeo's stand at the 1997 Earl's Court Show, despite the fact that Alfa GB was showing off the new 156 saloon for the first time. Out of 10,000 serious inquiries, 7,000 asked to test-drive the new model.

(Below) Beautifully proportioned lines of the latest Spider make it probably the most striking looking sports car of the mid-1990s.

Under the bonnet was a revised cam-cover, and most significantly, the Bosch Motronic injection system. The specification of the classic Spider was now up to date, although the Twin Spark motor was never on the cards.

trailing edge of the boot-lid and rear wings. Like the US versions, the new bumpers were fairly hefty items, and it was generally felt that they did the car few favours.

The updating process of the 2000 Spider was taken to its logical conclusion in 1985, when it was dragged further into the contemporary styling morass with the acquisition of a full-width front air-dam and embryo side-skirts. Apart from the lack of a roll-cage, it would not have looked out of place running in Class E in the SCCA's race series. Sold alongside the regular Spider Veloce and basic Graduate models – in the States at any rate – this top-of-the-range car was called the Green Cloverleaf or Quadrifoglio. It could be ordered with a matching factory hard-top complete with a heated rear window, and came with a full leather interior, electric windows, state-of-the-art stereo radio-cassette player and air conditioning as standard, plus the 15 x 6-inch 'telephone-dial' alloy wheels shod with 195/60-section tyres. The following year, the interior was further uprated to provide new seats and door panels, with a return to

the single oval binnacle for the main gauges, and a revised central console.

By this time, some people thought *anno domini* was beginning to catch up with the Spider. Writing in *Autocar* in January 1988, Neil McIntee relived his own graduation experience by returning to his old university with a Spider, remarking that: 'On the motorway, the car was showing its age. As might be expected of a car conceived a quarter of a century ago, refinement is not one of its strong points. And after an hour on the motorway the constant engine and exhaust noise, the wind buffeting the hood, the wind noise and bump-thump, were beginning to take their toll.' But in its defence, I have to say that it is, after all, a sports car, and that was par for the course, even in 1988. It can't have been all bad, however, because the writer vowed to own a Spider one day. And when he got on to the sort of roads where the car excelled, he could change his tune. 'You can feel everything the Spider is doing through the steering wheel and the seat of your pants. It has to be driven, and driven hard to gain the full benefit', he said. 'The simple but supportive seats, steering wheel and gear lever are in perfect relationship to each other, and there's plenty of room.' So far so good, then. I can endorse much of what he said, apart from the ergonomics bit.

Manufacture of the 105-series Spider reached its peak in 1986, when 7,015 units were built. The lowest point on the production scale was back in 1967, with just 2,962 cars leaving the factory. In 1988, the one-hundred-thousandth Alfa Spider rolled out of the Pininfarina works, but not long after a serious fire at the plant halted manufacture. Something like thirty days of production were lost, leading to a shortage of cars on the market and, just as worrying at the time for classic Spider enthusiasts, a hiatus in the flow of spare parts. The last of the be-spoilered square-tail cars were the models affected, for the facelifted car was just around the corner.

LEAN MACHINE

It was felt by many that the lean shape of the original Spider was compromised by the spoilers and skirts of the 1983 facelift and the mid-eighties Quadrifoglio. But actually, if you were to take the Quadrifoglio out of context, forget it had a past, and drop it straight in among the body-kitted car park of the late-eighties and early-nineties, it would look absolutely spot-on. It's only because the earlier cars, pre-1975 big-bumpers, looked so good that the body appendages appear odd.

Whatever your view, there is no question that with the comprehensive facelift of the 1990 model, the stylists at Pininfarina managed to restore some of the athletic character of the original boat-tail Spider, at the same time bestowing upon it a much more contemporary presence.

Styled in the Pininfarina studios by Sergio Pininfarina and Renzo Carli, and first revealed at the 1989 Detroit Show, the facelifted car's front panel combined to be the bumper, valance and Alfa grille all in one, and the back bumper flowed neatly into the rear valance. There was the slightest hint of a lip on the trailing edge of the boot lid, but it was part of the pressing, not an add-on. Gone was the clumsy hacked-off square tail, to be replaced by a more contemporary rounded posterior carrying the strip of Alfa 164-style rear lights.

However, plenty of the traditional features were retained in the revamp, principally the recessed headlights, the rounded and recessed door handles, and the flutings along the car's flanks. Even the dash was familiar, with the key gauges grouped in the binnacle ahead of the driver. The driving position was better and the seats were improved with suedette centre-sections and convincing leatherette outer panels likely to make for better wear and tear. Considering the Spider was virtually hand-built, its UK list price of £16,500 was extremely competitive when ranked alongside other hand-built cars like the Morgan Plus Four, which at the time was £15,104, before ordering galvanised chassis, aluminium panels and so on.

US-spec cars have had catalytic converters since 1978, but now all Spiders got them. This led to a small drop in power output, from 130bhp down to perhaps 120bhp, but the European Spider now ran with the latest Bosch Motronic ML 4.1 fuel injection and ignition system, and what it lost in power was easily compensated for by the smoothness of the delivery. It was not as inclined to rev as the Twin Spark motor of course, but it was considerably more civilized than engines breathing with carburettors or the Spica set-up. Purists, however, may have missed the sucking noise of the

The interior of the facelifted 1990 model was completely worked over, with re-shaped seats and door panels, a new dash, console and switchgear, up-to-the-minute instrument binnacle and a contemporary leather-rim wheel.

Webers or Dell'Ortos, which at least gave the driver the impression the car was trying hard. The torque curve of the 1990 Spider's twin-cam was enhanced by the adoption of an improved version of the late Alfetta's variable valve timing, whereby the cams were rotated by an oil-driven pump in relation to the position of the crank.

But the updating process could only go so far. The last of the classic Spiders could not be fitted with the then-new Twin Spark engine, because its restyled cam-cover was roughly 2in (51mm) taller than the existing 2.0-litre engine, and there would need to be a bulge in the bonnet to accommodate it. And the second distributor which, in the contemporary Alfa 75, was mounted ahead of the engine, would have projected into the space occupied by the Spider's radiator and fan.

With electric windows and a factory hardtop as standard, this car cosseted like no other Spider had done. It was almost difficult to appreciate when taking the wheel of a 1990 model Spider that underneath, it was still a 1960s concept, which may have

99

The successor to the classic Spiders was launched in 1995, inheriting much of the charisma of its ancestors. The incoming Spider's all-new chassis and drivetrain quickly earned the plaudits of the motoring media.

been ahead of the game then, but whose only real concession to the present was the incorporation of power-assisted steering. The British motoring press universally welcomed its return to the UK market place. *Car* magazine described it as 'comfortable..., un-temperamental and stylish. It has lots of go, and it's fun.'

Alfa Romeo GB at last had sufficient confidence in its long-suffering standard bearer to resume importing it, although it was still necessary to look elsewhere for right-hand-drive cars. It would cost an extra £3,000 to have the steering wheel moved to the right-hand side of the car, but having driven a number of Bell and Colvill's converted cars over the years, I could find no fault with them. A hiatus in the launch of the current

Spider meant that Pininfarina had to modify the last of the classic Spiders for sale on the US market, which meant fitting passenger air bags.

A NEW BROOM

The new generation Spider was to be based on the second series Alfa Romeo 155 saloon platform. Modern technology enabled all the tricks to be incorporated into the new car, including the new Fiat-derived version of the Twin Spark engine. But would this be enough to supplant the classic Spider, whose straightforward purity of design, plus a dependable mechanical formula, kept the 105-series car in the limelight for almost three decades?

3   The New Spider

Alfa Romeo's new Spider was introduced in 1994 and first imported into the UK in May 1996. Rumours of the new Spider and GTV had been circulating for some time before their launch, and when I worked as a sub-editor on *CarWeek* magazine in 1993–4 the magazine carried several stories and artists' impressions of the new models which had been gleaned in or leaked from Italy.

Alfa's engineers had to get the successor to the original Pininfarina design right first time, and the visuals we saw certainly looked promising. Magazine staff had access to the new-at-the-time front-wheel-drive 155 press cars, powered by the 1.8- and 2.0-litre Twin Spark engines, which gave us a clue as to how the new Spider and GTV would feel. But the thirty-year-old icon, which, by the time production came to an end, could claim global sales nearing 120,000 units in all its different engine guises, had set a number of serious precedents. While production volumes were relatively low, it had been a high-profile standard bearer for the company. So it would certainly be a hard act to follow.

Alfa Romeo had developed the new Spider and GTV as two distinct models – the two-seater convertible Spider and the two-plus-two GTV coupé – in order to appeal to quite different niches within the sportscar market. While the similarities in their design were inescapable, both models did indeed manage to project their own quite separate identity. This was undoubtedly a major triumph for Pininfarina and Walter

The new Spider was launched in 1994, although persistent leaks in the motoring press showed in advance what Alfa had in store.

da Silva at Fiat's Milan-based Centro Stile, for not only had they produced two striking shapes from a single concept, the new Alfas were easily as good, if not better than the new wave of contemporary sports car designs. They were right up-to-the minute, yet still contrived to contain a number of Alfa Romeo's traditional styling cues.

Alfa Romeo and parent Fiat could afford to be in optimistic mood. Their new flagships followed in the wake of the recently introduced 145 Cloverleaf three-door hatchback and 146 TI five door fast-back, and looked set to make a significant contribution to Alfa's sales growth and increased market share, particularly in the UK. Here, sales rose by a dramatic 77% in the first two months of 1996 compared with the same period of the previous year. The Italians' level of commitment seemed deeper than in the days of the old Spider, and now, of course, the new models were factory engineered in right-hand drive for the British and Japanese markets.

Not long after their launch, the new Spider and GTV soon won a number of design and styling awards throughout the European media, including from Britain's *Autocar* and *Car* magazines and the prestigious Golden Steering Wheel award in Germany.

Having a new set of clothes is one thing, but the *Alfisti* hoped that the appeal of the

The arresting new Spider and GTV were built on the Tipo-derived floorpan of the front-wheel drive 155 saloon car.

The 1995 Spider's lines were an amalgamation of styling input from Pininfarina and Fiat's in-house Centro Stile department at Turin.

new Spider would be much more than just skin deep. Both models were to be powered by the brand new version of Alfa Romeo's 2.0-litre four-cylinder twin-cam, twin-spark engine, now with four valves per cylinder. Always a brilliant motor when it powered the 75 saloon, it could now justifiably be considered to be up with the state-of-the-art engines. Some of the purity of the classic all-aluminium twin-cam was lost, in so far as the block was now cast-iron, but it was reckoned to be stronger for the switchover. Notwithstanding the implied weight increase, all the right elements were there: the 1970cc unit incorporated two spark plugs and four valves per cylinder, variable valve timing, hydraulic tappets, the latest generation Bosch Motronic

engine management system, a steel crankshaft with eight counterweights, and counter-rotating balancer shafts for refined running.

It had a relatively modest power output of 150bhp – up 20bhp on the old twin-cam – but 90% of torque was available at just 2,500rpm. Fuel consumption was relatively good, emissions were naturally well within regulation limits, and the Spider and GTV were endowed with a maximum speed of 130mph (210kph) and a 0–62 mph (100kph) acceleration time of 8.4 seconds.

Alfas have always been about the driving experience. Other makes like BMW are always touted as being better made – and I have owned and driven a number of them – but I believe their advantage in the build

The second generation Lotus Elan of 1990 has a more steeply raked windscreen and pop-up headlights, but in general, its nose-down, tail-up rounded styling is reminiscent of the new Spider.

Most prominent styling quirk is the crease that picks up the line of the front panel and bonnet joint, and runs diagonally upwards across the wing and door, to create the plastic hood cover.

quality department is negated because they lack the essential soul of an Alfa. It would be interesting to see whether the new Alfas could improve upon their predecessors. The handling and ride characteristics of both Spider and GTV centred on their new shared chassis design – located on the shared Tipo-derived floorpan of the 155 model – that incorporated an entirely new multi-link rear suspension system. This was anchored to a moulded light alloy sub-frame set below the floorpan.

As we shall see, this relatively advanced system was calculated to promote maximum tyre contact with the road, particularly when the car was cornered hard. It aimed to exploit the transverse loads generated by the steering that generate body roll.

Above all, sports cars need to be strong on chassis rigidity, and true to form, the high torsional rigidity of the Spider's body shell made a significant contribution to its handling characteristics. Alfa Romeo calculated that it would take 40,000kg/

Frontal treatment of the Spider majors on the Alfa heart-shaped grill and longitudinal air intakes, while the twin headlights were voted 'Best Design Detail' in 1995 by Car *magazine.*

Comparisons with other cars are inevitable, and it is clear what influenced Daewoo to produce its Joyster concept model, shown at Earls Court in 1997.

radian to produce torsional deformation between the front and rear axles of the Spider.

Other notable engineering additions included the quick, competition-proven high-ratio sports steering rack, which needed just 2.2 turns from lock to lock. To match the cars' performance, a powerful Bosch 5.3 four-sensor ABS anti-lock braking system, with a split hydraulic crossover circuit, was installed. This incorporated big, servo-assisted ventilated front discs of 284mm (11in) diameter, and 240mm (9.4in) discs at the rear.

SAFE AND SOUND

Safety features have always been something of a cliché, a yawn even, but the older one gets and the more impersonal driving becomes, what with road rage and motorway madness, the more sensible it seems to surround oneself with at least the minimum safety kit. These features were not lacking in the new Spider. Indeed, they were one of the priorities for Alfa's design engineers. They had to aim to produce a rigid body shell – always critical in a convertible – along with the ability for it to absorb kinetic energy. So they built in 'measured deformity' crumple zones to ensure maximum protection in the cockpit.

The front section of the body shell was designed to crumple and deform into a protective shield for the rigid safety cage, affording maximum protection for the occupants in the event of a head-on collision. The front struts were designed to collapse in a programmed fashion, thereby reducing and absorbing the force of any impact that occurred to the side or at the front of the car. Boxed sections under the floor were designed to absorb any impact forces from the subframe to which the engine is mounted, while cross- and longitudinal beams were used to strengthen the two-layer floor and minimize deformation of the pedal box. There was also a solid bulkhead between cabin and boot, which would protect occupants in the event of a rear impact and also shield the fuel tank. The A-pillars were reinforced to provide head and neck protection in the event of an inversion.

The fascia and other cabin furniture had rounded-off shapes with no protruding edges, and soft, yielding components calculated to lessen injuries in the event of an accident. Occupants were protected from lateral damage by the side-impact bars, energy-absorbing linings and recessed seat-belt housings.

The telescopic steering column was also billed as a safety feature. Its lower section incorporated a sliding sleeve, which would absorb any movement if the steering box was shunted, while the upper section was corrugated in order to deform and absorb the force of the driver's body if there was a crash. Seat-belt pre-tensioners that recoiled seven or eight centimetres in a few milliseconds restrained passengers.

The dual air bags were made of PA 66 artificial fibre, with a capacity of 55 litres for the driver and 120 litres for the passenger. Full inflation would take 20 to 30 milliseconds. They could operate even if the car's own electrical supply failed, because each airbag had its own power reserve. The Spider's on-board fire prevention system consisted of an inertia switch on the fuel-feed circuit, which cut off the fuel pump in an instant, causing pressure in the fuel lines to fall. In addition, a flow-stop valve located downstream of the petrol tank prevented fuel from circulating in the pipes in the event of an accident. The petrol tank and fuel lines complied with European Union 1997 regulations, while the upholstery complied with stringent US

High on Alfa's priority list for the new Spider specification were safety considerations such as crumple zones to provide a protective cell for the cockpit.

Alfa Romeo Spider 2.0-litre Twin Spark 16V (1994 to date)

Bodywork	Monocoque stress-bearing structure
Engine	
Type	Four cylinder in line
Position	Front transverse
Bore x stroke	83 x 91 mm
Displacement	1970 cc
Compression ratio	10:1
Max. power output	150bhp at 6200 rpm
Peak torque	138lb/ft at 4000 rpm
Fuel	Unleaded (95 RON)
Structure	
Cylinder spacing	90 mm
Main bearings	Five
Cylinder block	Cast-iron with counter-rotating balancer shafts
Cylinder head	Light alloy
Timing	
No. of valves	Four per cylinder, overhead in 460 V shape
Timing	DOHC, with electro-hydraulic variable valve timing
Timing control	Toothed belt
Valve clearance adjustment	Automatic, with hydraulic tappets
.Ignition	
Type	Static, electronic digital combined with injection, knock sensor, four HV coils and two spark plugs per cylinder
Firing order	1-3-4-2
Fuel feed	
Petrol pump	Electric, immersed in fuel tank
Injection	Bosch Motronic M2.10.3 Multipoint electronic combined with ignition
Air filter	Dry-type with cartridge
Emission control	Three-way catalytic converter plus lambda probe
Lubrication	
Type	Forced-feed with adjustment valve and oil/water heat exchanger
Filter	Cartridge

(continued...)

Cooling

Type	Liquid cooling, with forced circulation by centrifugal pump and sealed circuit; radiator and supplementary expansion tank
Control	By thermostat
Fan	Electric with thermostat

Transmission

Clutch	Dry, single plate, with contact bearing and hydraulic control; diameter of driven plate:228.5 mm; clutch lining dimensions (ODxID):228.5 x 155 mm
Ratios	1st: 3.545:1; 2nd: 2.238:1; 3rd: 1.520:1; 4th: 1.156:1; 5th: 0.946:1; Reverse: 3.909:1
Differential assembly	Front, in gearbox
Final drive	Cylindrical, 3.562:1(16/57)

Braking System

Type	Discs front and rear, with floating callipers. Pedal control, with split-line diagonally linked hydraulic circuits, vacuum servo, effort-proportioning valve on wheels and ABS as standard
Ventilated front discs	Diameter: 284 mm; total front lining area: 200 cm2 (asbestos free)
Rear discs	Diameter: 240 mm; total rear lining area: 84 cm2 (asbestos free)
Hand brake	Acting on Rear-wheels; manual control, mechanical operation

Suspension

Front suspension	Independent, MacPherson struts with lower wishbones and anti-roll bar
Front wheel geometry unladen	Camber: -1∞14í + 20í; caster: 3∞20+ 30í; toe-in: 0 - 2 mm
Dampers	Hydraulic, telescopic, dual action
Rear suspension	Independent, multi-link with upper wishbone, double lower arms, passive Rear-wheel steering, coil springs, hydraulic dampers and anti-roll bar.
Rear-wheel geometry unladen	Camber: -0∞55í + 20í; toe-in: 0 + 2 mm

Wheels

Rims	6 J x 15" light alloy or 6.5 J x 16" light alloy
Tyres	195/60 ZR 15 or 205/50 ZR 16
Inflation pressure	Front/rear: 2.3 bar/2.1 bar
Spare wheel	
Rim	4Jx 15" steel
Tyre	T 125/80 R15 96M
Inflation pressure:	4.2 bar

Steering

Type	Rack and pinion with power steering
Steering column	Collapsible with dual adjustment
Turning circle	10.8 m
Steering wheel turns	(Lock to lock) 2.23

(continued...)

Electrical equipment

Voltage	12 V
Alternator	100 A
Starter motor	1.4 kW
Battery (capacity)	70 Ah

.

Internal Dimensions

Waistline width	1336 mm
Elbow-room	1382 mm
Headroom 945 mm	
Centre brake pedal to lower edge of steering wheel	568 mm
Seat travel	200 mm
Steering wheel to front seat squab	560 mm

Boot dimensions

Height	530 mm
Max. width	1050 mm
Length	230 mm
Volume	110 dm3 (3.8 cu ft)

Weights

Kerb weight (DIN, full tank, spare wheel and accessories)	1370 kg. Distribution: front, 61%; rear, 39%
Weight fully laden:	1630kg. Distribution: front, 55%; rear, 45%
Max. payload	260kg
No. of seats	2

Performance

Top speed	130mph
Speed with engine at 1000rpm in fifth gear	20.9mph
Acceleration	Standing start, (2 adults + 20 kg (44lb)) (sec): 0–62mph (100km/h): 8.4; 0–1,000m (1,100yd): 29.8
Official fuel consumption	56mph (89.6km/h): 45.5mpg (6.21ltr/100km); 75mph (120km/h): 36.2mpg (7.81ltr/100km); urban cycle: 27.1mpg (10.4ltr/100km)

Production

Produced	1994 to date
Quantity	8,000 units per year

The rear-three quarter view of the Spider is like no other car. The dramatic crease from hood cover to front panel almost suggests that the top section of the car can be lifted off.

flammability regulations.

As flagship models, the Spider and GTV featured the latest and best that Alfa could throw at them. They were, after all, chasing a much larger audience than previously, so equipment levels had to be generous. Gone were the days when the sports car enthusiast was expected to sacrifice creature comforts for driving pleasure. For instance, nowadays the world and his wife swan around with aftermarket alloy wheels on their Vectra, so both GTV and Spider were also available with big 16-inch alloy wheels. They also got central locking, power

steering, height and reach – adjustable steering column, fog lights, electric windows, heated door mirrors and a stereo radio-cassette player. Air conditioning and leather upholstery could be found in the optional 'lusso' pack.

An adjunct of automobile safety is the security aspect. If you've ever had a car stolen or broken into, you'll sympathize with these concerns. Once, we left a party at an inner city location late one night, far from home and with baby in Moses basket travel mode, only to find the GTV6 was missing. And another time we lost a radio

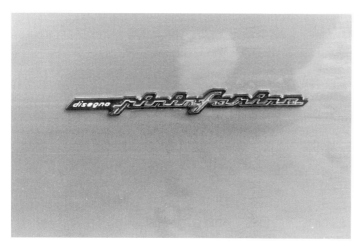

The Pininfarina logo is now so reduced that it is virtually indecipherable.

out of a 75 Twin Spark while it was left in a rural station car park, and I guess we probably got off lightly. There was nothing we could do about the deranged nocturnal attacker who set about a line of parked cars down our street, putting out the 75's headlights with a baseball bat. Thankfully for us, his principal target was a Golf GTi. The factory addressed issues like these by fitting the latest security feature as standard equipment, known as the Alfa Code ignition key. It performed by activating the car's immobiliser system through a transponder concealed in the key grip, which sent a signal to an aerial coiled around the ignition switch. The transponder emitted a code – known only to the driver – which was picked up by the aerial and activated the immobiliser control unit, which in turn froze the engine management computer, so that the engine could not be started without the correct key. This Alfa Code key was said to be difficult for thieves to copy, with some 20,000 permutations exclusive to Alfa Romeo.

In addition to its immobiliser system, the Spider was fitted with a remote-control ultrasonic alarm, programmed to go off in the event of forced entry. As an additional theft deterrent, Alfa GB went a step further. Prior to sale, all windows were etched with the Vehicle Identification Number (VIN) and eight-digit vehicle chassis number, and each vehicle was automatically registered with the National Vehicle Security Register (NVRA). Even the radio was encoded, and had a removable front panel.

DESIGN BRIEF

'Alfas? Do they still rust?' is the line you usually have to jump over when they ask you what you drive. After all these years, people haven't forgotten. Having just had to get a couple of bits of structural welding done on my current 75, now ten years and 145k miles down the road, I have come to be evasive. But with the new models, Alfa Romeo could lay to rest once and for all its legacy of corrosion that had drifted into folklore. Along with the rest of the range, the new Spider came with a comprehensive warranty package, including an eight-year corrosion warranty, a three-year paint warranty and a three-year/60,000 mile (96,000 km) mechanical warranty.

While the Spider and GTV were identical in design from the front bumper to the A-pillar – or windscreen if you prefer – it was from this point that the stylistic differences were evident, reflecting their differing roles. Naturally it was vital to incorporate the Alfa shield shape, and this, together with the inset badge, was the key feature at the front of the bonnet. Among the traditional Alfa design cues which were revived prominently were the air intakes on either side of the central shield, harking back to the coachbuilt 6C 2500s and 1900s of the post-war era. The ribbing on the bonnet converged on and drew attention to the badge, while the car's wedge shape, culminating in the relatively high cut-off tail, had become an Alfa hallmark. The deeply incised lines in its flanks were also evocative of Alfa models of the more recent past, like the 75 and 164 saloons and the dramatic SZ ES30.

There are similarities of thought in the styling of the Alfa Spider and the little Fiat Barchetta, launched in 1995, and this is hardly surprising since both emanated from the drawing boards of Fiat's Centro Stile. But I have to say though that the

Cockpit of the Spider is suave without being overly sophisticated or particularly adventurous. Everything works as it should, but the wiper delay system proved perplexing.

115

Being an open-top sports car, the Spider could also qualify for the appellation Barchetta – or 'little boat'.
The rear three-quarter view clearly demonstrates the slash in the bodyshell, running from hood-cover
to front bumper.

closest precedent I could find for the Spider's rotund wedge shape was the Peter Stevens-designed second-generation Lotus Elan, which was launched in 1990. Like the Spider, it was a front-drive car with a wide, rounded shape and steeply raked windscreen, with a similar flip-up cover for its soft top housing. There were naturally some differences in detail though, most obvious being the Hethel-built car's pop-up headlights. Its strictly two-seater bodywork was all glass-fibre of course, rather than just part composite. The Elan became the Kia Sport, of course, while another Korean sports car, which I perceived to be a dead ringer for the Spider, was the Daewoo Joyster. This was displayed as a concept car at Earl's Court in 1997, but was destined for production a year hence and likely to be a serious contender in the Spider market. It was styled and produced entirely at Design Forum, Daewoo's Seoul styling studio, the company's first stand-alone sports car study. Its clean, ovular lines and minimal overhangs, lights that were integrated into the wing fronts, were mirrored in an austere cockpit. It weighed just 900kg (1,984lb).

It was as clear as daylight where the inspiration for the Daewoo's front-end styling had come from, egg-crate grille or not. Of course, all cars have a 'face' of some sort, and the new Alfa Spider's face was its ace. Radically new, and positively avant-garde, are the pairs of double polyelliptical headlights, which, one discovers when lifting up the bonnet, are simply the lens elements of regular-sized headlights and not the torch-sized units that the tiny round apertures might lead one to suppose.

The other frontal feature of the Spider and GTV was the central air intake, set low enough on the car to be partly obscured by that wretched UK licence plate. The trapezoidal bumper that curved gently

With its soft-top in place, the Spider loses none of its rakish solidity, and if anything, it complements the lines of the car. The rear-light panel is nicely integrated between boot lid and bumper section, while the third brake-light set in the hood cover is a neat touch.

around the sides of the car integrated the whole arrangement of grille and air intakes. Both models were discreetly badged with a small Pininfarina badge on their rear flanks, just ahead of the rear wheel arch. From behind the A-pillar though, the two models took on their own distinctive identity. Along the flank of the GTV, as on the Spider, the steep groove extended steeply upwards to the high sawn-off tail, while on the Spider the tail fell away in a less radical and morestreamlined shape. This even managed to replicate the styling of the last of the classic Spiders, those with the post-1989 facelift.

The treatment of the rear section of the cars above the waistline also differed. While the GTV featured a large, steeply raked window incorporating a third stop light at its base, practical considerations meant that the Spider employed a hinged, body-coloured plastic hood cover. This item, which we shall come to in Chapter 6, blended quite well with the body and also contained a third stop light. Each car was badged simply with Spider or GTV in chrome identification on the boot lid, while the Alfa badge logo also served as the swivelling cover for the boot lock mechanism.

MANUFACTURING TECHNOLOGY

The Spider and GTV were built entirely at Arese, where the workforce numbered 6,000. (This included those involved in production of Alfa's V6 engines as well.) They were geared up to make 8,000 Spiders and 7,000 GTVs annually. While robots played a key role in welding and assembly of the body panels, both models were relatively low-volume and therefore clearly more labour intensive to produce than the 156, of which yearly production was set for 130,000 units. By way of comparison, Fiat

made 11,000 Barchettas and 20,000 Coupé models every year.

The design and manufacture of the new Spider's bodywork was innovative as far as Alfa and Pininfarina were concerned, and their adoption of new and unfamiliar technology in the manufacturing process played a key role in the creation of the bodywork. The result was that the bonnet, radiator grille and part of the wings combined to form a very neat one-piece structure. The Spider bonnet consisted of an inner frame and outer skin, which ensured that the structure remained absolutely rigid and would retain its

Boot space is about par for the course in a sports car, since the space-saver spare wheel, which also houses the jacking equipment, takes up much of it.

With the composite double-skin bonnet raised, the location of the Twin Spark motor can be seen right between the front wheels. It becomes apparent that the neat 'pin-head' lights actually emanate from large sealed-beam units.

original shape over time.

Clearly, it would have been extremely difficult to achieve the required shape for this assembly in sheet steel, so a composite material known as KMC, consisting primarily of polyester resin and carbon fibre, was used. Apart from specialists like Caterham, Lotus and TVR, other manufacturers including Alpine Renault and Porsche have used composites to good effect. They have several advantages over steel, such as the ability to absorb minor impacts without incurring damage, and panels that are more easily repairable, as well as being resilient and completely corrosion-free.

Two different formulae of resins were concocted to manufacture the KMC composites. One mix was for the outer skin to produce a steel-like appearance for the car's exterior, and the other, which was used to construct the inner frame, contained additional additives that could endure mechanical stresses and resist very high temperatures.

Both the inner and outer skins were moulded separately, using the compression injection process. This involved injecting the resin into a chromium-plated steel die heated to a temperature of 150-degrees Centigrade. The two halves of the die were then clamped together, compressing the injected material and forming the bonnet shape in the process. This polymerization took a mere 40 seconds. After that, a conductive primer was injected into the skin, covering its surface to a depth of around 100 microns. This layer of pigment formed a perfect base for the undercoat, prior to the application of the finishing coat by an electrostatic painting process. Finally, the bonnet frame and outer skin were bonded together, using a structural epoxy adhesive.

INTERIOR ERGONOMICS

Predictably, the interior design of both models was biased towards the driver. Both Spider and GTV shared the same fascia, majoring on rounded shapes dominated by a central vertical console. This section consisted of four ovoid niches, containing all the minor gauges that were angled towards the driver, the ventilation controls and outlets, and the radio-cassette player. The console flowed neatly – but nothing like as adventurously as, for example, TVR's – into the transmission tunnel area. Here were located the leather-clad gear lever,

Driving position is excellent, with both main dials housed in a central binnacle and auxiliaries angled towards the driver. Window controls are on the end of the door-pull / arm-rest, while leather-rim wheel-boss contains an air bag.

handbrake lever, cigarette lighter and ashtray.

The main instrument panel was directly ahead of the driver, mounted in a single binnacle on the top of the rounded dashboard fascia, shrouded from reflections by its deeply curved hood. It contained large circular analogue dials for the speedometer and rev counter. A small panel set between the two dials housed warning indicators for seat belt, air bag and door status together with a liquid-crystal mileage display and trip-counter. Additional panels at each side of the speedometer and rev counter housed switches for the front and rear fog lights, fuel cap cover release and trip-counter reset. The GTV's switchgear also catered for its rear window de-mister.

Apparently the driving position can be adjusted for both reach and rake to the leather-rim four-spoke steering wheel, which has the Alfa Romeo badge at its boss. I say 'apparently' because I failed to discover this facility. The delivery driver who brought the press car claimed there was no such adjustment when I asked him, but of course I should have investigated further. However, there was little to complain about with the Spider's seats, as they were certainly more comfortable than those of most previous Alfa Romeos. They were heavily bolstered for good lateral and under-thigh support and fully adjustable for reach and seatback angle. They also featured an anti-submarining cushion design, which prevented the occupants from sliding beneath their seat belts in a heavy impact. In addition, the seats were fitted with rigid head restraints, shaped to protect the spine from whiplash in an accident. The car I tested was clad in the optional leather upholstery, which I liked but my wife Laura did not. Along the top edge of the door panels was a finishing strip that extended the line of the fascia and housed the door

Pininfarina and Fiat's Centro Stile produced two striking shapes from a single concept, and Alfa Romeo projected the new Spider and GTV coupé (seen here) as two distinct models in different market niches.

handle at its leading edge. All storage cubby holes are valuable in sports cars, and at the base of the Spider's door panels were rigid storage pockets. Electric window control switches were located neatly at the top of the door handle armrests, with controls for both sides set in the driver's door-pull.

Just a Top Up, Please

Behind the Spider's cockpit was a recess that housed the fabric soft-top. This aperture was covered by a hinged semi-circular plastic cover, painted in matching body colour. The hood folded away into the body and was completely unseen when the plastic cover was fastened down. An American firm that also worked for Cadillac designed the Spider's soft-top. Some hoods do the shape of the car no favours, but in this case the hood managed to combine an attractive appearance with aerodynamic efficiency and a degree of acoustic comfort. However, the forte of the Spider's hood was its practicality, as it was very quick and easy to raise and lower. Its mechanism was specially developed, and consisted of a five-hoop steel and aluminium frame, and a soft-top consisting of a double-layer covering. The outer layer was in flame-retardant multi-ply fabric, which met both EU and American standards, and an inner layer in material with soundproofing properties. The front hoop was shaped to line up with the upper edge of the windscreen, and Alfa implied that this actually optimized the Spider's aerodynamic performance with the hood up.

Specially shaped quarter-light support channels were designed to reduce aerodynamic noise at high speeds when the car was driven with the hood up, and the plastic rear window was attached to the outer canvas by a zip-and-Velcro system for easy removal and replacement if needed. This reminded me of the time when I was presented with the keys to a Dodge Viper while I was on the *CarWeek* staff. Access to this unexpected bonus proved difficult, as the battery for the door lock 'plipper' was kaput. So, not to be outdone, I spent some time pacing around the car pondering how I was going to gain access to it. Happily the side-windows were on the similar zip–Velcro principal, and having undone one, I was quickly into the beast and away. Soft-tops have always been vulnerable, but this does not exactly encourage confidence in the security aspect.

The Alfa Spider's hood mechanism also incorporated gas springs, which were designed to minimize the effort required in raising and lowering the hood. In fact, these loads never exceed 10kg (22lb). There were also spherical hinges designed to permit variations in hood width depending on whether it was up or down in order to optimize use of the available space. The top was locked in place by a pair of self-centring pins at each corner of the 'canopy', to guide the front and rear hoops home, while a hook system automatically released the rear hoop and opened the hood cover. This was actuated by two electro-mechanical button-switches located in the right-hand side of the hood recess. A manual system was on hand if the automatic system failed. I have illustrated the procedure for its erection in Chapter 6.

Multi-Link Rear Suspension

Perhaps the most outstanding feature of the new multi-link rear suspension system was its rear-wheel steering capability, and it is worth examining the concept in some detail and seeing how it manifests itself in the way the Spider behaves on the road. Rear-wheel steering implies an ability to exploit the transverse loads generated by the steering that normally trigger roll. In

The Spider hit the bright lights in 1995, and took pride of place on Alfa Romeo's stand at the 1997 Earl's Court Show, despite the fact that Alfa GB was showing off the new 156 saloon for the first time. Out of 10,000 serious enquiries, 7,000 asked to test-drive the new model.

principal, the Spider's multi-link rear suspension optimized the working angles of the back wheels, helping to stabilize the car so that it could cope with rapid changes of direction when required, as well as enhancing tyre grip into the bargain.

The rationale for the new set-up was based on straightforward tyre and suspension technology. Each tyre can only yield its full potential when it is perpendicular to

The Spider's rear deck gleaming beneath the bright lights of Earl's Court, showing off its impeccable shut lines.

the road surface, and its grip and predictability reduces as it gets tilted towards either edge of its tread. Also, the reinforcing belts within the tyre prevent the tread from stretching along its length. As the tyre rolls, it generates longitudinal vibrations, which are transmitted to the car

through the suspension mechanism. Introducing compliance solves the vibration problem, but it can also lead to a lack of sensitivity, accuracy and responses in the car.

As we know, suspension componentry has two separate tasks. One is to keep the wheel and tyre as nearly perpendicular to the road as possible, especially when the car is rolling about its longitudinal axis during cornering. At this point, some of the weight is taken off the wheels on the inside of the corner, and transferred to the wheels on the outside of the corner. The other function is to ensure that the wheel is correctly steered, and this is true of the rear wheels as well as those at the front. It is easy to forget that rear wheels seldom point straight ahead, because in reality they are always subject to a certain amount of flexibility and lateral movement. In cornering, the effect is more pronounced, and the outer rear wheel is forced upwards against the resistance of its spring, relative to the car body.

With all this in mind, Alfa Romeo's engineers designed comparatively little elasticity into the rear suspension bearings, which each of the arms linking the wheel-hubs pivoted on. Each bearing was lined with a rubbery polymer carefully formulated and shaped to give the necessary degree of stiffness in each plane. Some of the longitudinal vibration could be dissipated in each of these pivots.

Then the engineers went a bit further. The pivoting arms were not connected directly to the body shell, but were located on a subframe. This in turn was mounted to the body shell by further rubberized fixings which allowed the subframe itself to move fractionally in the fore and aft plane, although vertically rather less so, and in the lateral plane hardly at all. The concept was that vibration could be damped out much more effectively if the task was performed by degrees rather than all in one go. The rear suspension's subframe was itself a state-of-the-art piece of engineering. Italy had always been among the world leaders in die-casting technology, and Alfa engineers embraced a new die-casting technique known as thixo-moulding, which

actually carries a Swiss patent. Here, fine grain aluminium was injected into a mould in semi-solid form, at 550 degrees Centigrade, to produce castings with excellent mechanical properties. This was particularly useful because the subframe was not only to serve as a vibration-absorbing device, but also as the stable platform from which all the suspension components had to perform. It was also some 10kg (30lb) lighter than a welded structure would need to have been.

The Spider's rear suspension hubs were mounted on a sturdy carrier, with pivots at the top and bottom. From the top bearing, a 'Y'-shaped arm extended in towards the car, and its forked arms pivoted from two bearings fixed to the subframe. From the bottom of the hub carrier, two diverging arms extended inwards to similar pick-up points on the subframe. One arm operated on the coil spring, the other on the damper unit. The upper and lower arms were not quite parallel, and they were not of the same length. Thus, when the wheel was forced upwards, its top became slightly tilted inwards. The Spider's multi-link arrangement exploits that slight tilt, serving to keep the wheel upright rather than allowing the tyre to be tilted on the road and thus diluting some of its cornering performance.

The phenomenon whereby the lateral forces developed in cornering were harnessed to help steer the rear wheels worked in this way: the two lower arms did not converge onto one single pivot at the bottom of the hub carrier, but each stopped short, at its own bearing. Slight swivelling of the two arms allowed the hub carrier to rotate about a point further out than that to which either of the arms extended. And those arms were of the right length to perform in the vertical plane. The swivelling was determined by another link, which connected the front of the hub carrier to the subframe, and this is the one that did the 'steering'. It was altogether a clever evolution of the concept of passive steering, as adapted to a sophisticated double-wishbone suspension system. Whether it worked satisfactorily in practice is revealed in Chapter 6.

The Spider and GTV front suspension was a far more conventional affair, as seen on other cars in the range. It employed independent MacPherson struts, with lower wishbones and an anti-roll bar. Apart from that, its only notable features were offset tapered springs and segmented dampers, intended to reduce the transmission of noise into the cabin and lift the comfort factor slightly. The Spider's five-speed manual gearbox drove through the front-wheels, and incorporated an anti-vibration system on the left-hand half shaft.

THE TWIN SPARK ENGINE

At the heart of the new Spider was its new 2.0-litre 16-valve Twin Spark engine. The light-alloy 16-valve twin-plug cylinder head was unique to Alfa Romeo, and unlike its 'classic' ancestor, the current car had its power plant mounted transversely in the engine bay. Now though, instead of the all-alloy unit that powered all classic Spiders and latter-day Twin Spark models, the new engine used a cast-iron block. Perhaps we should not be too surprised by what at first glance seems to be a retrograde step, because after all, the 1994 BTCC-winning 155 of Gabriele Tarquini used an engine that was an amalgam of Fiat parts-bin components. Assembled by the Abarth competitions department, it was basically the iron block of the 164 Turbo and the head from the four-wheel-drive 155Q4. Technology moves on apace and modern steel is as light as aluminium. As an example, try comparing the weight of a modern chro-moly steel

mountain bike frame against an aluminium one, and you'll find there's not a lot in it. The steel engine block is an improvement because it has higher tensile strength than aluminium. As we shall see later, the driving experience proved that its reputation for smooth power delivery, rapid responses and mechanical refinement was well justified. Just as significantly, the new Twin Spark engine requires no attention – other than oil changes – between 100,000km servicing. No spark plugs or timing belts to worry about: just drive it.

The Twin Spark motor was once described by *Autocar* magazine as 'probably the finest four-cylinder engine in production today'. They may not have been exaggerating, as this latest incarnation of the venerable twin-cam concept was undoubtedly at the cutting edge of production engine technology. It was also used in the contemporary 155, 156, 145 Cloverleaf and 146 ti, and was a member of the modular family of Alfa engines built at the company's new Pratola Serra plant at Avellino, south of Naples, which came on stream in 1997. The aim there was to exploit modular construction in the interests of a more streamlined and efficient production process. Engine capacities ranged from 1.4- through 1.6- and 1.8- to 2.0-litres. Interestingly, the new factory was built on the site of the old Arna plant, scene of the short-lived joint venture with Nissan in the mid-1980s to hybridize the Cherry Europe model with the flat-four motor of the Alfasud and 33.

This is how the Twin Spark engine worked. Each combustion chamber had two platinum spark plugs, but they were of different sizes and performed different roles. The larger one was central, and fired the compressed charge at the beginning of the power phase. The smaller one was offset at one end of the chamber and sparked 360-degrees later at the end of the exhaust

The Spider was available in certain markets with the fabulous double-overhead cam 24-valve 3.0-litre V6 engine, which gave the car a potential 150mph (240kph) maximum speed and 0-62mph (100kph) accelera-tion time of 6.7seconds. Performance aside, it was worth having simply for the aural delights it provided.

phase. This had the effect of both reducing emissions and protecting the catalytic converter by ensuring that no unburned fuel could reach it. Each cylinder had its own direct-ignition coil, and the spark plug leads were arranged so that the output from each coil was directed to two different cylinders.

Like the classic Alfa twin-cam, the Spider's Twin Spark engine was an in-line four-cylinder unit with two overhead camshafts. Now, though, in this latest version of the Twin Spark, the camshafts controlled four valves, inclined into each combustion chamber. Alfa's latest variable valve timing system was developed in consort with the latest electronic engine management system. The camshafts' relative timings could alter to vary the amount of overlap between the exhaust and intake phases. The phase shift was actually slightly less than in the past, a matter of 25 degrees instead of 30. But it moved to give full overlap at as little as 1,800rpm, when maximum torque was wanted, eliminating overlap at idling speed or at full power.

Variable valve timing works in conjunction with the electronics system, which handles the precise metering of fuel and ignition timing, as well as modulating engine knock, monitoring emissions, and governing the exhaust gas re-circulation system. By this means, the Spider's engine reached a brake mean effective pressure of 172.5 lb.ft/sq. in. This is the only true measure of how efficiently an engine breathes and burns its air and fuel, and it was an impressive figure when you appreciate that the Twin Spark engine was not designed to give a peaky power delivery. In fact, it maintained at least 90% of its maximum torque with a wide-open throttle throughout the speed band, from as low as 2,500rpm up to 6,200 rpm. It would even tolerate full throttle from as little as 1,500rpm.

Among the Twin Spark's technical attributes were hydraulic tappets with drainproof circuits to prevent knock, abolishing the need for periodic valve clearance adjustment. There was a staged, sequential static ignition system and the twin coils were built into the cylinder head. The Bosch Motronic M2.10.3 engine management system not only controlled the ignition and sequential indirect injection system, but also modulated the variable valve timing operation, controlling knock by adjusting advance separately for each cylinder, and governed the exhaust gas re-circulation system, or EGR, built into the cylinder head. The knock control system was active and selective for each cylinder, achieving peak performance for minimum specific fuel consumption by keeping the ignition advance close to knock level but

without actually allowing knock to take place. A heated throttle body with an electromechanical idle actuator ensured prompt response from the engine and smooth power delivery, while a water–oil heat exchanger maintained oil consistency during long periods at maximum speed.

Four-cylinder engines are inherently less well-balanced than sixes, and following Porsche's example with its 944 model, Alfa introduced two contra-rotating shafts into the Twin Spark motor to iron out the alternating moving masses which had caused the imbalance. The automatic tensioners for timing and balancer shaft belts were designed to be maintenance-free over extended mileage usage. The crankshaft now carried eight counterweights and a torsional vibration damper, and the cast-aluminium alloy sump stiffened the engine and gearbox assembly by having six securing points instead of the usual four.

GREEN ISSUES

As we have seen, Alfa Spiders were no strangers to environmental controls, especially those exported to the US. The latest Spider addressed these issues with its three-way catalytic converters and heated lambda probes. The lambda probe ensured that the catalyst operated effectively even after a cold start, minimizing pollution during the critical engine warm-up period. It had a head start in that the latest 2.0-litre 16-valve TwinSpark engine was designed for optimum combustion efficiency. In addition to its stainless steel exhaust manifold and exhaust gas re-circulation equipment, the shape of the combustion chambers was configured for peak volumetric and thermal efficiency in mind. Its two spark plugs per cylinder also helped reduce emissions. By the mid-nineties, Alfa could

The powerplant of the new Spider was the 16-valve Twin Spark motor, now using an iron block and aluminium alloy head instead of the all-alloy engine fitted in classic Alfas – including those using previous incarnations of the Twin Spark unit.

claim with justification that only fully recyclable materials were used in production and that its factory processes were subjected to regular ecological audits. A percentage of Spider production was test-driven around the company's Balocco site near Turin to ensure quality was up to scratch.

THE MARKET PLACE

In the UK, the new Spider was pitched into a niche of the market which was not only in the process of expansion, but which was fiercely competitive. It was a niche where badge chasing was rife and feelings about brand loyalties ran high. The sportscar and coupé sector, known in the trade as Segment H, was going through a period of healthy growth in the UK and throughout Europe during the early 1990s, although the rest of the car market was generally stagnant. Segment H may be small in volume terms, but it nevertheless has a strong influence on all other market sectors. It is a

diverse world, too, with products ranging from the Caterham Seven to the BMW Z3, and Fiat Coupé to the Jaguar XK8.

In 1994 this sector was dominated by the Ford Probe and Vauxhall Calibra, which accounted for almost 30% of sales. Although the MGF got off to a fair start with 851 units delivered, the Vauxhall Tigra (which, incidentally, looks from the back very similar to the MGF) accounted for much of the segment's overall growth during 1995 with 6,787 units, making it the best performer of the group. Segment H covers saloon derivatives from the 'worthy but dull' category such as the BMW 3-series Coupé and the Rover 200 Coupé, as well as cabriolets like the Saab 900 Convertible, Audi Cabriolet 2.0E, and the TWR-designed Volvo C70 convertible. But the Alfa Spider's real competitors are the true sports cars. These include the 'mass-produced' models like the Mercedes-Benz SLK and BMW Z3 as well as cars from specialists like Morgan, Marcos and TVR. There would also be a degree of customer overlap between

Alfa's own products, although the GTV and Spider have different purposes. Alfa Romeo identified the key target audience for the Spider as being evenly split between men and women in the AB socio-economic group, and within the age range of 35 to 55 years. Alfa Romeo reckoned that the size and presence of the Spider were likely to increase its desirability to those who found most convertibles in the category unappealing. In line with the convertible market, most UK sales were anticipated in the south-east of the country. Curiously, they also anticipated that the 'more obviously assertive nature' of the GTV would attract a predominantly male ownership. However, at least one female friend of mine has expressed a definite preference for the aesthetics of the latest GTV Coupé over the Spider. But quite frankly, as long as she buys one or the other, then I shan't mind a bit.

Although the Spider and GTV were identical up to the windscreen, the sleeker rear-quarters of the GTV Coupé contrasted with the flatter aspect of the Spider's tail.

4 Filling the Gap – Privateer Importers

Alfa Spiders might have been produced consistently for the past forty years or so, but they have not necessarily been distributed on that basis. For instance, where the manufacturers have not provided the concessionaire with stock to sell, one or two independent concerns have stepped into the breach.

During the past three decades, Bell and Colvill have been among the best-known Spider vendors in the UK, selling and servicing Spiders at a steady rate from their garage in picturesque West Horsley in Surrey. On several occasions Bobby Bell has been kind enough to lend me a Spider for magazine features, and when I told him I was researching this book he provided some interesting insights into the buying and selling of Spiders. His role was particularly significant during the period when the cars were not officially imported, and it would otherwise have been a Spider-less Britain.

Bell and Colvill first took on an Alfa franchise back in 1970 when they were making the first of the 1750 square-tail models. There were very few cars about then, according to Bobby Bell, and although he and Martin Colvill were the main Alfa Romeo dealers for the region, they sold hardly any Spiders until 1971, when the first of the 2.0-litre cars came over. Thereafter, they did very well until 1978, when the last ones to be imported came in from South Africa, which was a curiously indirect route – rather like Caterham's 1700 Supersprint motors. There were about 200 of them, and they were the last of the factory-made right-hand-drive cars.

Bobby Bell reflected that at the point of stopping making the Spiders in right-hand-drive form, Alfa Romeo were actually doing incredibly well in the UK, selling around 10,000 cars a year, of which the majority were Alfasuds. However, it has to be remembered that in the late 1970s, there were still a lot of British-made open-top sports cars available on the home market, from Triumph and MG as well as low-volume specialists like Jensen, TVR, Lotus and Morgan. Consequently, Alfa Romeo was not terribly interested in converting just a couple of hundred Spiders a year for sale in Britain.

Bell and Colvill prospered with them though, partly because they were also well known sports car specialists, dealing in cars like Elans and the bigger Lotuses. Around that time, Alfa Romeo GB issued their dealers with a questionnaire asking how many Spiders they thought they could sell, and the response was so derisory that they decided not to bother importing them. There was also another factor in play. Legislation was forcing manufacturers to tighten up on vehicle safety, with headlight heights affecting ride height settings and bigger and better bumpers, plus the possibility of items like rollover bars becoming mandatory. It was difficult to predict how far the crusade would go in the safety-conscious United States, and what aspects would overflow into the UK.

Nevertheless, Bell and Colvill carried on dealing in second-hand Spiders. Demand was still firm, but the number of cars available was diminishing. There was an obvious solution. Bring in new models from the Continent and convert them to right-hand drive. By 1983, they found there was sufficient interest and enthusiasm from customers to begin the process of convert-ing and supplying right-hand-drive cars. Bobby Bell admits that their first attempt was 'slightly tacky', but they put it in the showroom just to show what could be done and, sure enough, it was soon sold. There-after, they cajoled their subcontractors into gradually improving the quality of the con-version. The first ones they operated on were finished like factory cars, with pedals coming up through the floor, but they sub-sequently changed the pedal installation to a pendant mounting. 'The factory-produced right-hand drive Spiders' brake system was a bit of a disaster,' claimed Bobby Bell, 'because all the brake pipes were under-neath the car where they corroded, as did the master cylinders, and the pivots would seize up. They also had a twin brake servo system, with the master cylinder under the floor and two remote brake cylinders under the bonnet. In some people's view it is an absolute nightmare to bleed this system, because you cannot tell whether it is the master cylinder or one of the servos that is faulty. The factory never actually sorted out a less complicated set-up.'

The final assembly of Spiders has moved around, and they were assembled at Arese during the late-seventies. Most recently, the classic models were completely built at the Pininfarina factory, but the fire of 1989 made it more difficult for Bell and Colvill to get cars. They employed an agent, who located cars for them, and they did not deal directly with Pininfarina. They cannot even be approached about supplying spare parts, because their role is that of subcontractor, and everything is referred back to Alfa Romeo.

OPERATING THEATRE

Bell and Colvill's methodology was straightforward. Once they had the vehicle back at base, it was straightaway converted to right-hand drive. The operation was not too difficult, 'provided you were geared up for it', explained Bobby Bell. 'Since you couldn't get right-hand-drive steering boxes, the existing one had to be swapped over and mounted in a cradle on the right', he said. 'The steering idler had to be cut and re-welded into the right position, and of course pedals, controls and wiring had to be swapped over.'

It seemed that the only componentry that could not be switched was the left-hand drive wiper system, so a small amount of visibility was lost if the screen was particularly dirty. Their subcontractor became sufficiently practised that the conversion was performed very quickly, and from 1985 to the advent of the new Spider, almost a hundred a year were converted, with a price tag in 1987 of £15,495.

Bobby Bell went on to muse that Alfa Romeo has always come out with limited production runs, like the 105-series chas-sis-based Montreal V8, which occupied a niche unfilled by any other Alfa sports-GT car, the replica 4R Zagato and, more recently the 'Monster' ES30 SZ. He deduced from this that the Italians love limited edition sports cars, and that 'some of their manufacturing is from the heart rather than the wallet.' Since production of the classic Spider was only ever at the rate of four to five thousand a

One of the principals of Bell and Colvill is Bobby Bell, seen here with a freshly imported 3.0-litre V6-engined Spider – in right-hand drive, too.

year, it followed that these cars fell into much the same bracket.

The conversion business built up during 1984, and until 1986 there was just the one model, with twin-binnacle instruments, carburettors, and a choice of steel or alloy wheels. Then in 1986 Bell and Colvill began importing the Green Cloverleaf 'Quadrifoglio' versions, which had different instruments, and better sound deadening. Bell and Colvill offered the standard 2.0-litre car and the Green Cloverleaf 'Quadrifoglio' body-kitted car, with 15-inch wheels and low-profile tyres, and occasionally some 1600-engined cars. 'A few of the later

2.0-litre cars from Germany arrived without the engine-driven cooling fan', said Bobby Bell. 'It seemed they'd finally done away with that!' He thought it amazing that Alfa Romeo had persevered with it for so long. With the new Bosch fuel injection in 1989, drivability was improved, taking the power of the non-catalysed car up over 130bhp and making it an increasingly attractive prospect.

In 1989 the standard cars also had catalytic converters fitted, and now Bell and Colvill's Green Cloverleaf cars were imported from France and Belgium, and the non-Cloverleaf cars from Germany.

A fair number of US-spec 'dry-state' Spiders were imported into Europe in the late 1980s, and although they are less attractive visually – because of that giant wraparound front bumper – they can still win concours prizes. This is Martin Ellis with his 2000 Veloce, which lifted the 105-series Spider class trophy at the 1997 UK National Alfa Day.

This was mainly because the German importer was able to sell more of the standard cars and had a bigger allocation. Bobby Bell perceived two kinds of Spider buyers; there were the enthusiasts who preferred the purer, unkitted shape, and those who just saw it as a nice new sports car, with no real conception of its classic heritage. The latter would probably opt for the Green Cloverleaf model.

Although the Duetto with its long, rounded tail continues to be regarded by many enthusiasts as the prettiest Spider, Bobby Bell regarded it as 'a bit boat-ish', definitely more vulnerable and thus not as practical in crowded city streets. He thought the boat tail possibly generated turbulence at speed, and was almost certainly less aerodynamically efficient than the Kamm tail. 'It was probably harder to make as well', he observed. True enough, as restorers confirm that the Duetto shape is more difficult to repair, aside from the question of rear light, boot lid and other specific spare parts availability.

The arrival of the facelifted car in 1990 with its nicely rounded front and rear ends had marked something of a return to the original Duetto shape. It was certainly neater than the body-kitted Quadrifoglio, and a nicer car to drive as well. Bobby Bell thought the fitting of catalytic converters reduced the power output from 127bhp to 118bhp, but the car was so much more flexible with its fuel injection that it did not feel any slower. The power steering was well balanced so that, like its contemporary saloon, the Alfa 75, it loaded up the faster you went, while in town it was not necessary to employ armfuls of muscle to park the car.

Although some people were disappointed that the facelifted Spider did not have the TwinSpark engine, Bobby Bell felt that the regular 2.0-litre twin-cam in its 1990 guise probably had the right amount of power relative to its brakes and suspension set up. 'In any case', he pointed out, 'there wasn't room to install the deeper twin-spark motor with its double distributors in the Spider engine bay without resorting to bonnet bulges, and probably having to relocate the radiator header tank as well.' I reflected that there were no such inhibitions when they dropped the 1600 engine into the 101-series Giulia, or shoehorned the 2.5-litre V6 into the Alfetta GTV.

Bobby views the 1990 Spider as a well-balanced car, where the tail could be made to slide at relatively low speeds anyway. 'It's a safe, spartan sports car, which doesn't need any more power', he asserted. He cited the case of one of his customers, who had fitted high-lift cams to obtain more power, but who was still not especially enamoured of his car's performance, simply because he found he had lost out at the bottom end. 'You only get the benefit of high-lift cams and bigger carburettors at high revs, and if you look at the power curve of this sort of engine, up until 3,500rpm it's not doing much, and only really delivers at 5,000rpm', Bobby pointed out. A turbo-charger provides a much smoother and positive power delivery, once the notorious

'lag' has passed. Bell and Colvill became famous for their turbocharged Alfetta GTVs and Lotus Esprits towards the end of the 1970s, and they were a year ahead of Lotus themselves with the same application, so it is hardly surprising that they toyed with the idea of a turbocharged Spider. It would have been very quick and very lively, as was demonstrated by Reeves Calloway in the States, but, eventually, performance didn't enter into the marketing picture. They took the view that the turbo conversion and the necessary modifications would add an extra month on to the lead time for a car that already had to be located, imported and then converted to right-hand-drive.

'A chassis without a great deal of inherent grip can be made to go a lot more quickly with a turbo because the power comes in relatively gently,' Bobby said. 'And since it wouldn't spin its wheels in the same way as a car tweaked with cams and carbs, it could have been a better route to achieving more power for the classic Spider. But in the end, we decided not to bother.'

Even when Alfa GB began importing Spiders themselves, Bell and Colvill continued to import the cars. Then with the appearance of the new model Spider and GTV, a new market opened up. Not only did they source cars from other right-hand-drive markets; they specialized in importing the fabulous 3.0-litre GTV V6 model, which was not scheduled to come to the UK until mid-1998.

Apart from the Alfa Spider and GTV, Bell and Colvill also sell Lotuses – the very first Elise was delivered from West Horsley – as well as holding Saab, Subaru, Isuzu and Ssangyong franchises – and playing an active role in the classic sportscar racing scene. Martin Colvill was renowned for his Ford GT40s, and Bobby Bell's glorious 1971 Alfa Romeo Tipo 33/3 evoked memories of Group 6 World Sportscar Championship prototypes in action when it appeared at classic meetings like Goodwood and the Coy's Silverstone events.

SPIDER RACKETEER

Here is another tale of Spider importing, but this one is on a much smaller scale than Bell and Colvill's professional operation. During the mid-1980s, the craze for classic cars was at its height. Even Japan was not immune. The reasons for the rush to secure a piece of automotive history were largely two fold. Classic cars were more interesting to drive than ubiquitous hot-hatches, and their popularity ensured that they became fashion accessories. The rarest ones became financial investments, earning that dreaded epithet 'collector's car'. A rash of magazines sprang up on the back of the classics wave, such as *Restoring Classic Cars*, on which I worked for a time as Deputy Editor.

Such was the popularity of high-profile models like the Alfa Spider that there was actually a shortage of these cars on the market, exacerbated by the fact that many desirable vehicles had rusted away with the passage of time. The big auction houses like Coys of Kensington had always imported important cars, but now enthusiasts and entrepreneurs began rushing off to Europe, where classic foreign makes were cheaper and more plentiful, and to Florida and California to seek out the mythical dry-state, rust-free cars. The favourable pound–dollar exchange rate at the time helped a lot .

One such enthusiast was Dermot Golden, an Australian tennis pro who, until 1989, enjoyed a ranking alongside his sparring partner Pat Cash as one of the world's top professionals. Facing that difficult moment when all sportsmen and women have to look for a less strenuous occupation,

Dermot turned to importing classic Alfa Spiders for his new vocation. The experience was not all sweetness and light.

Importing cars looked like a good alternative to whacking tennis balls, but Dermot had been coaching in California and a lot of other places, and had decided on a Porsche 356 as his personal car to run around in between playing tournaments. In Australia and Europe these cars were prohibitively expensive, but in the mid-eighties he'd spotted one or two in southern California that were particularly cheap. However, sure enough, the next time he went back, they'd all gone; the Germans and the Swiss had shipped them back to Europe, apparently over the space of two or three years while the dollar was particularly weak.

An Alfa Romeo Spider seemed the next possible thing to Dermot, and he just missed the 'buy of a lifetime', having 'phoned the vendor and arranged to see his car at 9 o'clock in the morning. The trouble was, the seller had told a few other people to show up at the same time, and Dermot was beaten by a corpulent German, who ran up to the car pulling his money out and shouting: 'Sold! Sold! I buy it!' The deal was accomplished that quickly. Buying cars in California became so competitive, that it turned into a sort of 'Mad Max' race to outwit other potential buyers.

Dermot wasn't daunted by this, and after a few more days of hunting, he spied another Alfa Spider for sale. His bid was successful this time, and having bought the car he set about shipping it. However, the more he looked into it, the more he saw how complex and potentially hazardous was the procedure involved in exporting cars. He soon discovered that you must submit your pink slip and the car's entire documentation to the shipping company, and once you've handed over your car and your pink slip to the shipper, you effectively kiss

With the boom in classic cars in the late 1980s, Aussie tennis pro Dermot Golden turned to importing Spiders from California. Apart from all the hassles, the game turned up one or two surprises, like this 102-series Touring-bodied 2000 Spider. This model was produced between 1958 and 1961, during which time 3,443 units were made. It was recognizable by the twin bonnet air scoops, and sidelight-indicators in the grille-ends instead of the later car's driving lights

it goodbye until it arrives in England. Alarmingly, Dermot found out that the operators at one of these shipping companies had convinced forty or fifty people to part with the money to ship their cars, then closed their gates, sold off the cars and vanished.

He finally found a shipper who offered a reasonable deal, and discovered that for the cost involved he might as well pack two or three cars into one container. This was really the moment he decided to make a new career for himself as a classic car dealer. Ideally he wanted to keep one for himself and sell off the others, but once he'd actually got them back to the UK, the demand was so strong that he sold all three. Despite the ugly federal bumpers and smog

equipment, at around £5,000 they represented quite a bargain when rust-free examples were so scarce in Britain, and sound UK ones were fetching more than double that figure.

Back Street Crawler

Having given up tennis completely, Dermot went back to the States after some more Spiders. Now, in California, Alfa Romeo is not a marque that's particularly well known, and a lot of people steer clear of them. They are rare and relatively hard to find, but, even so, he soon ran into some dubious back-street traders: one Los Angeles dealer who specialized in Alfas tried to sell him two cars that were actually quite badly damaged. Dermot soon came to the conclusion that he was better off buying privately. His impression then shifted and he began to see that there were actually fewer cars available in California than there were in England. This was surprising, because the US was the principal market for Spiders. But it's a big country, and Dermot believes he over-reached himself.

If buying and selling Spiders was not to be the lucrative scheme he had hoped it would be, it did provide him with some interesting experiences nevertheless. Once he went to see an unspecified car some-where out in the desert near Las Vegas, and when he got there it proved to be an Alfa Spider. It was a non-runner, but not good enough to buy. It had a non-standard wind-screen wiper, and he asked the seller what the blade came off, and was told it came from another Alfa, a 'small thin fastback' in the wrecking yard down the road. So out of interest Dermot went to see what it could be, and there, ending its days just baking in the sun, was a Montreal. Another time he answered an advert for a 1959 'Alf' Romeo convertible. The seller had no idea what model it was, and claimed his brother had parked it up seven or eight years previously. It turned out to be a Touring-bodied 2000 Spider. And at the price he struck, it proved to be a very good buy indeed.

Now, having fun dashing round looking at cars in the West Coast sunshine carries more than a hint of glamour, and perhaps picking up a bargain or two is a way of making a living. But getting your treasure safely back to Blighty could be just as fraught with difficulties as it was in the time of the sixteenth century Spanish treasure fleets. Once the rigmarole of US shipping formalities was out of the way, the Atlantic crossing achieved and the cargo

landed in the UK, Dermot found that the hassles of getting his cars out of Felixstowe docks needed to be experienced to be believed. To get his Spiders off the quayside, once the authorities had deigned to uncrate them, they had to be towed. On one occasion the tow truck he'd booked failed to show up, another time it broke down, and a third company let him down a further three times. None of the local garages was inter-ested in helping him out. Hindsight is all very well, and he should have gone along with a specialist Alfa mechanic and the all-important towing vehicle. However, the first time he went to pick up one of the cars, he had no tools with him, and it proved to be a real problem to get it going, as the Duetto's fuel tank and carburettors were dried out because the shippers always suck the petrol out of the system in order to freight the cars with no fire risk. One way of getting the cars started after they have landed is to pour fuel into the tops of the Webers, and Dermot finally persuaded two workmen from the Stena Line machine shop to lend him the basic tools to do the job. Then at the dock he was charged £15 to pump up a flat tyre. It was a steep learning curve, involving quite a few salutary if elementary lessons. Der-mot never went to the docks again without his tool kit, a foot pump and a tow car.

The most infuriating revelation was that every shipment he made was damaged in some way. In each container, at least one car had been dented or scratched, had its hood ripped, or the radio stolen. The shipper's insurance policy was apparently designed so that the customer or car-owner would even-tually give up trying to claim on it. The claimant had to pay the first £250 anyway, and this sum, plus the damage repair bill, came off the profit. Dermot also found that the agents on both sides of the Atlantic were slow, and the containers regularly sat on the Suffolk dockside for six weeks, at the mercy of

Dermot had no problem with storing his cars. The author was able to accommodate them, and of course it was essential to start them up and turn the wheels once in a while.

the salt-laden sea breezes, when the handling and administration could surely be accomplished in two or three days. Dermot's experience in Australia was vastly different, where if a car sat on the quayside for longer than a week, the customer would feel entitled to make a considerable fuss.

Golden Rule

On the face of it, Continental Europe looked to be a better place to buy classic cars. One could acquire a car in southern Italy, Spain or Portugal, for example, and drive or trailer it back to the docks in France, Holland or Belgium, take it straight off the ship and through customs with no more than an hour or so delay. I once imported a classic Citroën via Zeebrugge with no hassles at all. The car is paid for, duty and VAT are settled, and the car has been imported without incurring the risks of careless handling.

One area Dermot had no problem with was storing the cars. I was in the fortunate position of having multiple garage space to spare at the time, so a succession of these dry-state cars came my way, and of course it was essential to turn the wheels once in a while. Not that they hung around for very long, though. But eventually, Dermot became disillusioned with importing Spiders from the US. Apart from the mechanical complications of California-specification cars with their catalysts and unloved and misunderstood Spica fuel injection, together with their unbecoming bumpers, he discovered there were so many Spiders coming through the docks that it was actually becoming a very common car, and in no time at all prices became depressed accordingly. Suddenly Dermot was hard pressed to make much of a profit on Spiders that now fetched only £4,000 or £5,000. They were coming into the UK from all over the place, such as Saudi Arabia, Switzerland, Belgium, as well as the US. A contributory factor seemed to be that the British will pay more for their cars than anywhere else in the world so, naturally, everyone would like to sell their car in Britain.

As for Dermot, he got involved for a short time in customizing Spiders, perceiving a big market for add-ons like the Zender body kit, which included side-skirts and a dam under the rear bumper. He thought it was a lot calmer than the late-eighties factory Quadrifoglio body kit, which he perceived to be too brutal and over-powering; he felt the Zender kit blended in better with the shape of the car. He was not alone, and firms like Lombarda operated a lucrative sideline improving the interior of the classic Spider with a walnut dash and upmarket seats and steering wheel. But Alfa Romeo's radical facelift for the model, coupled with the arrival of the new car, saw that particular niche for customizing coachwork take a serious downturn. So Dermot went back to a different kind of coachwork. Coaching tennis.

5 Restoration – The Legacy of Corrosion

There are several euphemisms for rust, even verging on the affectionate, such as 'the dreaded tin worm', or 'the creeping lightness', although why we should confer the slightest pleasantry on this destructive process is quite bizarre. As we now acknowledge, most cars of the 1960s and 1970s fell foul of the disease, but probably none more so than Alfa Romeo and Lancia. That they were probably not much more susceptible to corrosion than other makes was because only the top manufacturers paid any regard to underbody protection in those days. Also, it is in the nature of Alfas to be driven and enjoyed by their owners and whereas the average 1960s family saloon will have succumbed through corrosion and stylistic or technological obsolescence, an Alfa Romeo is likely to have been kept going, allowing the attendant rust problems to surface.

The legend of the adulterated steel used by the big three Italian manufacturers, imported cheaply from 'behind the Iron Curtain', may account in part for the premature rusting of some Alfa Romeos from the seventies. But corrosion could strike swiftly. Even in 1967, *Motor Sport* magazine had noted 'bad rusting of the hinges of the boot lid' of a Spider they had on test that had done less than 6,000 miles (9,600km). So this proves that they were always prone to rust due to being under-painted in the production process, and when subjected to the intemperate winters and salt-laden roads of northern Europe, they hadn't a chance.

One of the foremost practitioners of classic Alfa restoration is Mike Spenceley, who believes that in general, most of the Spiders' body-work problems can be applied to other 105-series Alfas.

A couple of Alfa Spiders await restoration at Mike Spenceley's MGS Coachworks premises. The Giulietta is still in paint, while the 2000 Spider has been stripped back to bare metal. The full extent of the work required will usually be revealed at this stage.

UNTANGLING THE WEB

Restorations are quite straightforward once the car is back to bare metal, and the extent of the rust damage can be inspected, but it's only when you start delving under the surface that you find all kinds of unseen difficulties. A few hours spent with practising restorers shows up the complexities and vulnerable areas of the Spider.

For the last three years, Mike Spenceley has judged the Spiders at the National Alfa Day Concours. Together with Jeff Sheridan, he runs MGS Coachworks in Purley, Surrey, specializing in first-class restorations of classic Alfa Romeos.

Mike Spenceley wears his considerable skills and talents lightly. He speaks with the quiet authority of someone who knows their stuff, and he doesn't patronize customers by pontificating at them. According to Mike, 'Alfa Spiders are not difficult cars to look after, providing that any remedial work undertaken is carried

out by someone who cares about what is being done, and understands what needs to be done and how to do it correctly.'

He identified the Spider's Achilles heel:

'The most difficult areas in these cars are the sills, and it's vital they're repaired correctly, because they provide the majority of the vehicle's structural integrity. Each side of the car has three separate longitudinal sill sections, which means that in any kind of remedial operation, all three should be dealt with – inner and middle sections as well as the outer ones. Ninety-nine percent of the cars that come through my workshop have had work done in the sill area. But the vast majority of them have only had work done on the outer sill, which is effectively just a cosmetic job. In these cases, serious rusting continues unseen, and superficially sound-looking cars can literally be falling apart from the inside. Clearly this makes them highly

Spider aficionados Chris Sweetapple (in car) and Andy Cameron urge caution when looking to buy a classic Spider. The very best ones are eligible for the annual AROC concours event, and among the prizes is the Andy Cameron Trophy for best Roundtail Spider.

dangerous, as the sills will have little strength in the event of an impact.'

The silver Spider 2000 featuring in the restoration shots was such a case in point. At some time in the past it had had new outer sills simply pop-riveted over the top of the rusty inner sills, and then had filler applied to complete the disguise. Before MGS Coachworks began work on the restoration, the telltale signs were evident in the rust bubbles at the bottom of the front wings, and the rust holes appearing in the rear of the inner wheel arches. Just how complex a job is the replacement and repair of the Spider's sills, wings and bulkhead is revealed in the picture sequence taken of this Spider during refurbishment.

Although Spiders represent a large proportion of his work, Mike Spenceley's heart lies more with the Giulia Super saloon, although his partner Jeff Sheridan drives a Spider. Of late, Mike has seen a great deal more interest in the Super/TI than ever before, although it has always enjoyed a major following in the Netherlands and elsewhere in mainland Europe.

Mike's comments on Spiders have a certain relevance for all classic Alfas.

'There are several other weak areas on Giulias and Giuliettas, although they are not structural and therefore somewhat less serious. But they do require careful examination and treatment as soon as possible. Potential problem areas are the lower front valance, including the cross-member for the radiator support; both lower ends of all wings, front and back; the inner wheel arches; doors and boot lid, spare wheel well, the soft-top's rear drain channels; the rear valance, and of course all jacking points.'

Potential owners should not be deterred though, and in fact Mike takes a heartening view: 'Although this probably sounds terrifying to the prospective Spider buyer, once the work is undertaken and carried out by a reputable restorer the car shouldn't need any further work.' That is to say, provided the owner then takes reasonable care of it; preventive conservation' is the buzz-word in the world of museums and galleries, and clearly it makes sense to apply it to classic cars by protecting your vehicle annually with Waxoyl. Get your friendly neighbourhood Alfa specialist to spray your car's innermost recesses.

'Once restored, classic Alfas should be no worse than any other car which gets subjected to the extremes of the British climate and the practice of spreading rock salt everywhere once snow and ice appears', said Mike.

When Spider restoration was at its peak a few years back, one of the first people I talked to was Chris Sweetapple, custodian of the British Alfa Club's 105-series register. Chris is the proprietor of the Highwood Motor Company in Swansea, which today specializes in original and reproduction replacement panels as well as most other componentry for these cars. He described some of the pitfalls of Spider ownership. When I expressed shock at the state of his own car, then in the throes of a major rebuild at Highwood's former Chelmsford workshops, Chris motioned me to what had once been a blue Spider. This

unfortunate vehicle was so badly rotted that it was impossible without detailed examination to determine its age, and, sure enough, although Chris's own car appeared in places to be a mass of patches, this blue car was so bad that hardly any panels at all could be saved. And the startling thing is, the blue Spider had apparently looked quite good on a cosmetic level before the Highwood team had started delving into its inner core.

As with a lot of cars, it is a case of 'not judging the book by looking at the cover', but it seems this may be especially so with the Spider. Chris had a word of warning to anyone contemplating adding a Spider to their stable: 'Unless you can afford a completely original car or one with a fully documented restoration, the best Spider to buy is one on which you can actually see the bad bits. That's to say, before the car has had any significant work done on it.' He has been around Alfa Romeos a long time now, and declared that the bodged Spider is a very common animal. When researching stories during my time on *Restoring Classic Cars* magazine, I came across no end of freshly uncovered bodges perpetrated on innocent Spiders. New owners were angry and heartbroken, as well as financially challenged by the prospect of big money restorations instead of the light cosmetic job they had originally envisaged. Generally speaking, where a restoration is being contemplated, all the old clichés hold true, and it's a case of 'look before you leap'.

Chris warned that the middle range of the Spider market was a particularly precarious area in which to go shopping. He felt that to be really sure of what you are getting, it is probably better to go for a cheap non-runner in need of restoration, as you would never lose money on it in the long run. I am not convinced this is right because, no matter how good the restoration, it is in the nature of cars to deteriorate and the job is going to have to be done again in perhaps fifteen or twenty years. So maybe it doesn't matter then; you buy the best you can afford. Values of Alfa Romeo Spiders have stabilized compared with the rapid escalation of the late eighties, partly due to the recession of the early nineties and the introduction of the new model. As I write this in early 1998, rock bottom for a classic Spider in the UK is about £3,000, less for a car needing restoration, of course, with tops about £15K. US-spec models are rated lowest of all because of their heavy bumpers and unknown Spica injection set-up. A thorough restoration is going to set you back at least £10K, so judge for yourself.

VALUE FOR MONEY

Another UK Alfa Club stalwart and restoration expert is John Timpany, who was once in partnership with Chris Sweet-apple. John now runs the Timeless Motor Company from more or less the same Essex location, specializing in overhauls and repairs. Back when he was half of the Highwood Motor Company, John renovated a fire-damaged Spider, bought for just under £3,000 and worth perhaps three times that figure after restoration. By way of comparison, I once saw a Spider Junior in a draeadful state, the metal of its wings now as fibrous as silken thread and its floorpans flaking like desiccated coconut, sold for £1,500 at a National Alfa Day meeting. But with a complete set of panels, this car could be back at a future event in concours condition and probably worth well over £10,000. It seems then that a restoration can treble the value of a classic Spider. However, it is more than likely that the restoration will cost the difference between the purchase price and the car's ultimate value. In fact, money spent on restoration is rarely recouped and you do it for the love of the car, although there are one or two specialist dealers like Tiverton-based Richard Banks who manage to put cars though top-quality restorations and still turn a profit on them. Richard Banks sells his cars to customers who can afford and appreciate the very best in Alfas. He does not condone Alfa Romeo motoring on the cheap, and has always been critical of owners and aspirant owners who are not prepared to spend money on their cars to buy the best or maintain them in tip-top condition.

The middle ground where cars are an unknown quantity and where buyers should be circumspect is between £4,000 to £7,000, because they could well be buying a host of problems. John Timpany observed that you would be paying so much more for your trouble in this price bracket. As an example of just one of the time-absorbing aspects of a classic rebuild, he indicated the characteristic Pininfarina fluting along the car's flanks, which is very difficult to retrieve in a restoration. (Interestingly, it was not unknown for customizers in the late 1960s to paint in this concave area with a contrasting colour: a white stripe on a red or blue car, for instance.) As Mike Spenceley attests, when the restorers strip the paint off a car, they find all manner of horrors. This may be an overly pessimistic view, but old hands like these have seen an awful lot of Spiders, so it's important to stress that what looks all right superficially, may in fact be none too brilliant underneath.

SOURCING PANELS

The facelift that took place in 1983 endowed the classic Spider with those comparatively massive federal bumpers, together with the front air dam or chin spoiler, and a rubber 'gurney' spoiler on the lip of the boot lid, which produced a more contemporary appearance. This was not particularly good news for the restorer, however, because although the panels for the mid-eighties cars might retain the overall shape, they are not quite identical with the pre-facelift models. For example, the mid-eighties front wings end at bumper level, so a panel would have to be made to span the gap between wing and valance. The rear wings on post-facelift cars have apertures into which the large wrap-around bumpers are mounted; the petrol filler hole is a slightly different shape, and the boot lid carries holes for mounting the spoiler. The inner rear-wheel-arch panels are also at variance and the apertures in the back panel for the rear lights are larger than before. All these discrepancies have to be compensated for, mostly by welding-in small patches, should the restorer be obliged to use modern 'federal' panels.

As far as original panels for pre-1983 Spiders are concerned, things have been getting pretty tight since the late 1980s, but excellent reproduction items from places like Highwood and Richard Norris do just as well. Check the Appendix for a list of sources and specialists.

A large number of Alfa Romeo enthusiasts and specialists obtain whatever new parts they need from EB Spares, who are based on the West Wilts Trading Estate, Westbury, Wiltshire. Alfa fans themselves, EB (The Italian Connection), as they call themselves, are the biggest independent stockists of Spider spares, certainly in Britain, and probably in the world. Anyone intent on maintaining their own Spider would benefit financially by dealing with EB Spares, for not only are their prices several percentage points cheaper than those charged by normal Alfa Romeo

franchises, you get the part straight away, or next day by mail order. This means you don't have to wait for weeks, and perhaps for the wrong part, a situation not uncommon a decade ago. With old Alfa franchises falling by the wayside and brand new ones starting up, there is little sustained awareness of the classic models, let alone continuous knowledge of the parts needed to fettle them. EB's altruistic attitude stems from a desire to see older Alfa models kept running, and to enable those of us

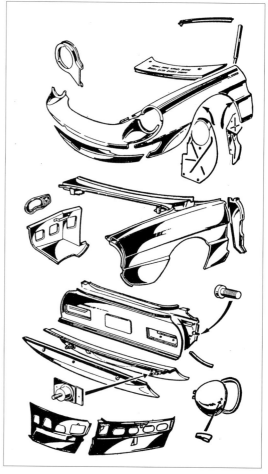

Exploded view of classic Spider's front and rear wings, valances and body panels.

without infinite resources to afford to do it. There is really no question of EB Spares treading on Alfa GB's toes, as they adhere to an agreement made in 1972, whereby EB will only stock parts for Alfas more than five years old.

The initials EB stand for David Edgington and David Butcher, and the firm was 28 years old in 1997. Edgington worked previously for Rob Walker's Alfa Romeo dealership at Corsley, near Warminster, Wiltshire, where he was assistant service manager by day and car salesman by night. Walker's was the most successful Alfa dealership in the UK, and visits from Milan were frequent. There were hectic times by all accounts, when Astons, E-types and cut-down Mini Sprints rubbed shoulders with Alfa Giulias, and even an unsold Ferrari 365GTC served as a loan car. Rob Walker was still a Formula 1 entrant in those days as well, which of course carried major kudos. David Edgington recalled that when the Duetto was announced, Alfa GB was desperate to offload any remaining 101-series Giulia Spiders, including some which had been stagnating in a warehouse at Folkestone for literally years. Even unsold examples at Corsley had moss growing on the window trim. How times change.

The other EB founder, David Butcher, worked as a mechanic on Jaguars and Triumphs at a local dealership, but he has long since retired from EB. His place was taken by Kevin Abigail, previously of another restoration and tuning firm, Benalfa Cars, who are not far along the road from EB Spares. In the mid-sixties, when concessionaires Alfa Romeo GB was a fledgling concern, an arrangement was made with Rob Walker for Corsley Garage to act as spares depot and suppliers for the whole country, and David Edgington quickly became parts manager. This, of course, is how he came to have such an intimate

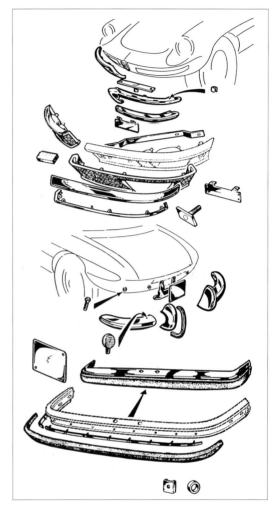

The 105-Series Spider's front and rear bumpers and light assemblies are complex, multi-faceted affairs.

knowledge of the 101- and 105-series parts numbering system. The Fiat takeover in 1987 did not help matters, because Fiat set about imposing its own parts numbering system on Alfa Romeo, and began phasing out slow-moving items.

In 1969, Edgington and Butcher set up their own company near Devizes, Wiltshire, dealing in new and pristine second-hand

The following sequence shows just how complicated the Spider's three-tier sill structure is, and how MGS Coachworks tackles its restoration. With offside wing and sill panel removed, the appalling condition of the inner wing bulkhead and front sill area are all too apparent.

The bulkhead has to be repaired in stages, with the rotten sections cut away and replaced with new metal patches.

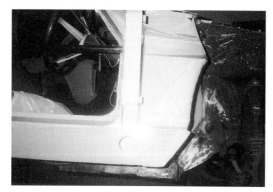

The offside inner wing bulkhead and middle sill areas are now repaired and painted with primer.

The inner sill section has been repaired and primed, prior to the middle sill being fitted. Note the hefty beam still supporting the door shuts.

The lower edge of the offside rear wing has been removed, and the inner sill has been fitted and primed. The middle sill will be fitted next.

The offside rear wing has yet to be repaired, but the middle sill has now been fitted and the inner wheel arch corner repaired, awaiting primer.

The outer sill panel has been fitted and the lower section of the rear wing repaired. Next step will be to fit a new front wing.

It is not always necessary to fit complete panels, as repair sections are available from specialists like Highwood, Richard Norris or EB Spares.

Head on shot of the Spider with lower valance, grille and Alfa shield removed, showing the repaired front cross-member.

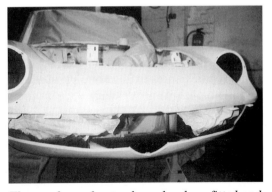

The new lower front valance has been fitted and the bodyshell is in primer.

Alfa Romeo components. So good were the used parts that EB felt able to offer full guarantees. This extended to a reconditioned gearbox service for 101- and 105-series cars, and with a move to Bradford-on-Avon, they sold cars on behalf of customers as well. By 1976, there had been another change of address, to the firm's present home at Westbury, and the trade in used and reconditioned parts was dropped. Now you can get only brand new parts and tuning equipment like camshafts and springs, which they import direct from Italy.

David Edgington naturally keeps a weather eye on spares for all classic Alfa models and compiles a 'doomwatch' for Alfa Romeo Owners' Club members, published from time to time in the UK club magazine. His appraisal of the situation is less gloomy for Spider owners than for drivers of the 105-series coupés, where panels in particular are very scarce. However, original Spider front and rear wings are nearing extinction, even in Italy, and rears are probably already unavailable. Rear inners, upper and lower front panels, rear valance and back panel are also rarities. Clearly there is not a lot left. Rear lights, splash panels, headlamp cowls, grilles and bumpers, and even fuel tanks, are in extremely short supply, and round-tail and Duetto rear lights are extinct. The positive side is that at least the more modern panels can quite easily be adapted, and some repair panels in good quality steel are available, including ones for the rear wheel arches.

PATCH OR PANEL

It is always going to be swifter and less messy to fit entirely new panels rather than welding in endless patches. You only have to balance the cost of panels against the time spent welding, grinding down and filling around patches, and see what the equation looks like. I paid a visit to another leading Alfa specialist, Benalfa, whose philosophy this seems to be, and talked to proprietor Alan Bennett about his methods of Spider restoration. Alan once worked with David Edgington at Rob Walker's garage, and some 20 years ago began doing work on Spiders in his spare time for EB Spares. Benalfa has been going for about 15 years, and at times the yard is full of Spiders, which tend to be mostly 1970s cars ripe for restoration. In the workshop you might find, as I did, anything from a beautiful Giulietta Sprint Speciale to a Touring-bodied 1900 Superleggera Coupé, plus a couple of boat-tail Spiders in restoration, with the odd 101-series Spider having its tappets seen to. Benalfa also carries out mechanical work, from engine rebuilds to performance tuning, and this includes head-skimming and reworking valve guides and seats. Indeed, most customers seem to like their cars refettled mechanically as well as bodily, and when the late Malcolm Morris restored my GTV6 race car back to road-going spec, the engine was rebuilt by Benalfa.

The company will also manufacture small components like bushes and do repairs on hood frames; in fact, Alan Bennett rarely turns anything away, and he gets Spider owners coming to him from all over Europe, and even from the US. Very often he finds himself rectifying mistakes made by 'do-it-yourselfers', but is happy to help them out. He has a poor opinion of the crop of cars imported from the US in the early 1990s, where fuel injection problems are rife and no Spica spares are available. It also appears that the average US owner (rather than the enthusiast) has run his car into the ground, with little regard paid to maintenance. And according to Bennett, the so-called rust-free California car is a myth, or at least, he hadn't seen one. On the legend of the adulterated Eastern European steel, Alan had an interesting story to tell. Apparently a customer of his who worked for Rolls Royce was in a position to analyse the window frames from a 1970s Alfasud, and he found no fewer than nine different metals present in the composition. Due to the fickleness of the chemistry they reacted against each other, and corrosion was the swift and inevitable result.

All the cars that arrive at Benalfa for bodywork restoration are in a poor state, to the extent that Alan is surprised when a car is actually not as bad as he thought it would be. First of all, he talks his customers through the restoration procedure, so that nothing is left to chance. But not until the car is cut apart can the true extent of the work required be appreciated, and when that has been done, it is often necessary to reassess the customer's aspirations for their car. The majority of people elect to go for the full treatment, but of course when they see that their pride and joy amounts to little more than a pile of rusty swarf, it's not a difficult decision to make.

The first job is to get the carpets out and remove the soundproofing, and then it starts to become possible to see which areas need renewing. We examined a late 1970s Spider whose owner had lost control of her car, and collected a gate and a hedge before going down an embankment. With masterly understatement, Alan said he thought she had been quite lucky, because the sills turned out to have been completely bodged and the strength of the car thereby compromised. The incident revealed that the whole rear nearside wing had a crazed appearance, showing it to have been entirely covered in filler, and to have been resprayed a number of times.

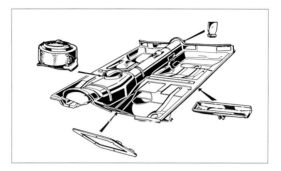

The Spider floorpan and transmission cover is common to all 105-Series models.

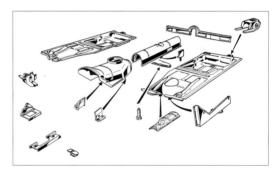

Exploded view of components that go to make up the the Spider floorpan.

The owner of the crashed Spider would probably have gone on to spend upwards of £8,000 for her rebuild, which included the price of the panels but no major mechanical work. This particular vehicle would be checked on a jig before repair work commenced to ensure there was no serious discrepancy in its geometry. In a similar incidence of slapdash repair work, an ivory-coloured Scottish car had simply had pieces of tin riveted over its existing sills.

Crucially, all the Spider's longitudinal strength is imbued in its sills. They consist of an inner section that joins the bottom lip of a big internal chassis member, which runs from wheel arch to wheel arch, a middle section and externally, an outer sill, which is the section visible under the door. The bottoms of the wing panels form the rest of the outer sills. Sometimes a good sign of the strength of the sills is evident in the door gaps, which if they are too big, indicate a 'banana' car – literally a bent monocoque – or too small, suggesting an abundance of filler. If possible, Benalfa carries out sill work with doors in place to preserve the shape of the body shell, while other restorers carry out this operation with steel poles bolted across the door aperture from hinge to striker plate.

A look inside rusted holes in the floorpan and sills of the crashed Spider at Benalfa showed that silver paper had been used to simulate the metal, and it had simply been back-filled to the appropriate level. Quite obviously there is no strength in that either, but bodges like this are very difficult to detect. So long as it seems to be solid metal, there is no reason for an MOT tester to probe any further. Benalfa makes up sections of floorpan to be welded in, to replace the rotten bits which have been completely removed. Boot floors are available for the 2.0-litre cars, and these are automatically fitted because the originals are inevitably a mess. There will be serious problems where the inner rear wing meets the boot floor, the back panel and the rear valance. Typical rust areas on the front inner wheel arches are at the start of the main box sections, running front to back, and adjacent to the spring mounting. An accumulation of mud around a scuttle drain channel will rot out the nearside inner wing at this point.

In a restoration, Benalfa reckons to replace absolutely every panel on 2.0-litre cars, from wings and doors, to sills and front and rear sections. For these cars, they adapt the current federalized panels, but with round-tail cars, they can only use 2.0-

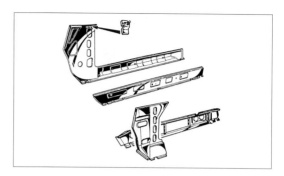

At the root of the Spider's body is the triple sill structure.

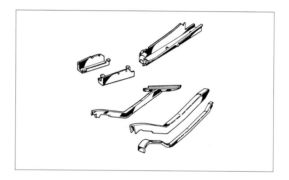

The 105-Series floorpan is buttressed by a number of bracing struts.

litre panels for the front half of the car. The back wings have to have wheel-arch panels and the lower wing portions rebuilt using one side of the car as a pattern for the other. The 2.0-litre wheel arch matches that of the round-tail car, and then the restorer works forwards to the sill and then back to the rear valance, which is made up and welded in. He uses 2.0-litre pattern wings and upper and lower front panels, modified to make up the heart shape for the grille. The front panel is then split and raised up to create the characteristic hump of the round-tail car above the grille. According to Bennett, not all restorers do this, nor do they all follow this methodology. One particular problem is the scuttle panel that

*Being an open-top sports car, all the Spider's strength is in its sills. If – or when – these rot, replace-
ment is essential. Before work can commence, it is vital to fit a brace across the door apertures so that
the car body cannot flex or go 'banana' shape.*

carries the windscreen wiper mounting
points. This is only available for left-hand-
drive cars, which of course is not ideal for a
right-hooker, as you lose a section of
windscreen visibility with the sweep of left-
hand-drive wiper setting. So Benalfa makes
up completely new scuttle panels.

The classic Spider's original finish was
either in synthetic enamel or what is
termed thermoplastic acrylic lacquer,
spray-painted in four coats to a depth of
between 78 and 140 microns. Over the
years, Spiders were finished in a number of
colours from the 105-series palette, with

red of two different hues being the most
popular choice, followed by white, silver,
petrol blue, light blue, Dutch blue, amaranto maroon, dark and pine green, ivory,
beige, yellow and yellow ochre. There were
three metallic options: olive green, silver
grey and light blue.

When all the metalwork has been sorted
out, Benalfa's Spiders are painted in two-
pack, as Alan finds there isn't the
inclination these days to devote sufficient
time and effort into the polishing of a
cellulose finish. And in any case, two-pack
is much more durable because of its resin

After all the new metalwork has been installed and ground down, undulations and blemishes are made good with filler. After this has been flatted off, the bodyshell will be primed.

The primer coat reveals further blemishes, which will be rubbed down. The car is masked up again and will remain like this at MGS Coach-works for several weeks before being painted in its finish coat.

A host of small inner panels and fixings make up the Spider's scuttle and centre section, through which run the drainage channels so crucial when it is wet and the top is off.

constituent. Finally, of course, the car is cleaned up to remove over-spray, and the customer's individual requirements are seen to, which might well involve a new hood. In the UK, the firm called T.A. and J.M. Coburn of Blunsdon, Swindon, Wiltshire, is the best source of Spider carpets, upholstery and hoods. Prices range from £214 for a set of carpets for a Spider (although costs vary for different models, and smaller sections are also available), to £644 for a mohair soft-top, supplied and fitted. They also do door panels with chrome trim as appropriate, headrests, seat squabs and cushions, hood bags and gear-stick gaiters. Considering the amount of

work that goes into making up car upholstery, those prices seem like pretty good value.

The one thing fundamental to Spider survival is drainage, and this is precisely why the sills are prone to rotting. When the car was built, the sills received only a thin film of black undercoat, so they are very vulnerable in any case. The innermost sill has a drain hole shaped into it, the intended drainage point for any water which gets into the two sets of drain channels located at the rear of the hood well and just to the rear of the doors. There may not be excesses of rainwater in Italy (which is arguable, having spent a week in the

157

The same 2000 Spider at MGS Coachworks is virtually unrecognizable now it is fully restored and in pristine condition, resplendent in its metallic silver livery.

Italian lakes one May,) but until global warming sets in for good, rain is a fact of life in the UK, so it has to be taken into account if your Spider is an all-purpose car. The problem is that the hoses that carry the rainwater away from the hood area terminate abruptly before they reach the aperture in the sill. Consequently, you will have water sluicing about within the sills, and if the drain hole becomes choked with mud, the water will never get out. An apt solution carried out by some restorers is to fit longer lengths of hose in the drain conduits, so that they actually protrude through holes drilled in the inner and outer sills and project out into the fresh air. That

way there's no chance of water staying around inside the car. At Benalfa, they underseal the sill panels before fitting them, and then underseal the seams when the weld is complete. They cut the new drainpipes off in their original place, maintaining that it is then only necessary to keep the drain holes clear. Then all cavities in the body are filled up with Waxoyl.

There's every chance that a well-used Spider is going to be caught out in a storm with the top down at some point in its life, which is why older Spiders, at least, had rubber mats instead of carpets. This was much more practical. There are two large rubber grommets under and behind each

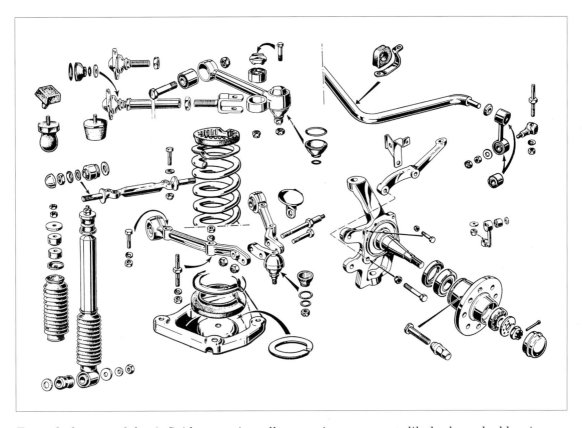

To get the best out of classic Spider motoring, all suspension components like bushes, wheel bearings and dampers need to be in tip-top condition.

seat to drain off the legacy of a major deluge, and unless your Spider has rubber mats like the Duetto, you'll want to get the carpets out from time to time to make sure they're not completely soggy underneath.

With any restoration, the mechanical bits can always be renewed, reconditioned or swapped. It is the bodywork that is crucial. Again, what is true for Spiders is virtually the same for all their contemporary saloons and coupé models. For example, it is common to find that dampers, track rod ends, kingpins and bushes need replacing, and spring pans can rot out. In my

experience with a Giulia TI, I found that the electrical system was the dodgy area, and particularly the lighting circuit, where bulbs were often blowing. Other weaknesses in the mechanical department include the bushes in the prop shaft universal joints; if you hear a curious rumbling coming from below the car when the engine's idling, that's what it may be. Burned out valves are not uncommon, and there is also a tendency for head gaskets to blow. I have had a couple go on Giulia Berlinas, and dropped a valve on a 1300 as well as a 2.0-litre Alfetta. In order to protect the head gasket the best advice is not to rev the engine hard until it has thoroughly warmed up. This syndrome is due to the aluminium block and steel wet-liners expanding at different rates when heating up, actually causing the block to shrink away from the alloy head. This allows oil pressure to blow past the six O-ring seals between head and block, to the detriment of the gasket. When the head gasket is renewed, it is advisable to have the head skimmed in case it has warped. Then keep it regularly serviced, use the correct Champion plugs (NGK make one that will suffice) and check the oil and water levels rigorously. Other mechanically sensitive areas on 105-series Alfas are the synchromesh on second gear, and there is a tendency to jump out of reverse. Clutches sometimes have to be replaced of course, while wheel bearings wear out perhaps faster than average, and again this can be recognized by the graunching noise

when cornering. Other areas to beware of are soft dampers, worn track rod end and anti-roll bar bushes, which should be in perfect condition to get the best out of the car. And though it may seem trite to mention this, running with the right tyre pressures also ensures optimum handling.

Finally, if you want to do your own maintenance or are simply interested in viewing your Alfa's anatomy, the factory manuals for the Spider and other 750/101 and 105-series cars are available now on CD-ROM. This facility was originally set up by the Dutch AROC, but Chris Sweetapple has the UK franchise and sells the CD-ROMs from his Highwood Motor Company for £53. They include sales brochures, owners' manual and workshop manual. Chris will send them worldwide on a mail-order basis and on 24-hour delivery in the UK. Alternatively, it is possible to access workshop manuals and tools through the Owners' Club and the Club shop.

6 The Driving Experience

The classic 105-series Alfa Spider and the latest model both have distinctive Pininfarina styling; both have excellent five-speed gearboxes and, mechanically, state-of-the-art twin-cam engines. For thirty-odd years, they have represented Italian styling and mechanical sophistication, and have generated a degree of romance that few other sports cars can match. So two decades on, what does a classic Spider feel like to

All aboard! String-back driving gloves were not absolutely necessary to get the best out of your 1750 Spider Veloce back in 1969, but they did help grip that slippery wood-rim wheel and shift the 'knife-through-butter' gear lever.

drive, and how much of a quantum leap is the latest car to bear the hallowed Spider name? Would they be as different as chalk and cheese, these Alfa Spiders?

Let's take the older model first. Having drooled over its beautiful lines and lowered yourself into the cockpit via the door – rather than doing a Dustin and vaulting aboard as if on a mission to find heart-throb Katharine Ross – one of the first things you notice is the gear lever. The classic Alfa's gearshift sticks out at you almost from the horizontal, and the gate seems to be more or less on a vertical plane, which is at first strange. What was considered in the 1960s to be the 'knife-through-butter' standard by which all others are judged, the Spider's shift is still just as mechanically precise and satisfying, but about half as fast as the modern Spider.

When doing the initial research for this book it was fortunate that my Spider-importing contact, Dermot Golden, was garaging a succession of his California cars at my house, and I had carte blanche to try them out, mostly on the local B-roads. To drive a classic Spider today is a pleasant reawakening. Supposing you have only driven modern vehicles for the last twenty years, the old-timer comes over like a breath of fresh air. Your initial impression of its handling might easily remind you of a

Track days and practice evenings on race circuits are an excellent way to hone driving skills and extract maximum performance from the car. These occasions are sensibly held in the summer months, but many Alfa drivers use their cars all year round.

The 105-series Spider chassis is lively by today's standards, and twirling it around the turns is a much more intense and involving experience than a modern car when you get it right through a set of bends. John Timpany's 1976 Spider 2000 leads at Lydden Hill.

skittish, nervous thoroughbred horse. If it's a Duetto or 1750, it's likely to be due to the car's narrow 165 x 14 tyres, which are a lot more responsive than modern rubber. The brakes have little of the positive firmness of modern anchors, let alone ABS, while on the move the steering feels light and the gear change wonderfully precise. The shift will feel slow, although it is positively slick compared with the shift of the transaxle layout of the interim Alfetta family. The

only thing to watch for with the 105-series cars is the downshift from third to second, as the synchromesh is likely to be worn; the selector-damaging graunch is best avoided by taking a little more time over the shift and double-declutching as you come down through the gears.

There may seem to be something odd about the pedals too. In all right-hand-drive and early left-hand-drive cars, the pedals pivot from the floor-mounted pedal box

The Alfa Romeo Owners' Club runs a comprehensive race series every season, as well as Autotests like this one at North Weald airfield, Essex, where David Dugdale is trying hard in his Giulia Spider.

rather than the pendant fashion that is more or less universal nowadays. Another aspect of pedal use is that you need to prime the carburettors with four prods of the accelerator pedal before firing up, and then delicately feather the throttle until the engine fires cleanly. Now that we've become blithely accustomed to fuel injection we've forgotten the idiosyncratic routines involved in starting carb-fed cars.

Once on the move, the Spider feels taut and composed, although the 105-series Alfa chassis is remarkably lively by today's standards, and there is a completely different kind of satisfaction as you twirl it around in the turns. It's a much more intense and involving experience.

Compared to a modern car, balancing the classic Alfa on tiptoe is far more satisfying, particularly if you get it right through a certain set of bends. It is so absorbing that you are literally dancing with it as it glides seamlessly through the bends, trimming its course with minute adjustments of the accelerator. There's none of the safe and secure 'cornering on rails' composure which you get with the current Spider. In the classic car, it's pressure off the throttle to create turn-in, and back on lightly to bring the nose out again, all the while playing with the wheel and gear shift as conditions demand. You soon become sufficiently confident to let the back end get out of shape, provoking it on purpose, just for the pleasure of gathering it up on opposite lock and bringing it back in line.

When stationary at a road junction or traffic lights, your classic Spider rocks nervously as the twin-cam's tickover pulses through it. Spider suspension settings are such that the car sits at rest with a slight nose-down attitude, switching to nose up, tail down under power acceleration.

GOING CLUBBING

One of the best places to try out a car is at one of the UK Alfa Romeo Owners' Club's practice evenings, held several times during the summer at Snetterton, Norfolk

and Castle Combe, Wiltshire, with track days at Goodwood and Aintree circuits. Here you can use the whole width of the track to slide the car if you care to, opposite locking like a racing driver. Power-wise, the full-on thrust and revability you'd get from a modern Twin Spark Spider are lacking, even with a 2.0-litre car, but nevertheless it is very entertaining.

Meeting up with like-minded souls is made easy through the Alfa owners' clubs, and they are unquestionably the best sources of information on parts availability and where to get repairs or maintenance done. There are Alfa clubs in most countries where the cars have a following, and it is worth mentioning the scope of the British

Area sections of the AROC participate in regional shows, such as the G-Mex Northern Classic Car Show in Manchester, where the North-West Section stand featured three 105-series models – Spider, Sprint GTV and Giulia Super – in 1987.

AROC's activities. It is co-ordinated by Michael Lindsay, who is Secretary as well as Editor of the Club magazine, and the Chairman is the indefatigable Ed McDonough. Like one or two other club stalwarts, they travel with their wives to events and race meetings all over the country and abroad, providing a unifying presence. Each of the classic models has its own register, coordinated by a member who is an authority in his field. The Club is sub-divided into regional sections that have regular monthly meetings, and there are organized outings for the Club as a whole, such as *Andiamo Milano*, organized by Ken Carrington and Chris Melville Brown. In 1997 this high-speed jaunt took in a visit to the factory at Arese, including a presentation on Centro Stile by marketing supremo Giorgio Pavia. It included lunch in Maranello with attendance at a couple of race circuits en route. Club members also organize other slightly less strenuous but equally entertaining events, like a swift dash around Scotland in the Carrera Pancaledonia, or maybe pop over to Holland for Dutch National Alfa Day. Or you could take part in the annual 200-mile Alfa run, or help project a national identity by staffing a Club tent at the important

Alfa fans fortunate enough to own pristine examples can participate in the Club concours events. Here is Basil Lamb's boat-tail 1750 Spider Veloce alongside an Elan Sprint in the final of the Scottish Classic Car Weekend Concours at Doune, 1985.

Even in club racing, all cars are fully prepared to race specification with appropriate suspension modifications, stripped-out interiors, full harness seat belts, fire extinguishers, roll cages and fuel tank protection, as Tipler found when he converted a GTV6 into a racer, seen here at Castle Combe in 1990.

Coy's Historic race meeting at Silverstone or a stand at the International Classic Car show. As well as the annual dinner dance, the undisputed highlight of the calendar for British Alfisti is National Alfa Day, staged in early June at Stanford Hall near Lutterworth in the Midlands. Here the aficionados and their families gather in force to talk Alfas over their picnic, drool over the concours cars, buy and sell, and take part in the gymkhana. Other similar happenings include Northern Alfa Day at Nostell Priory, and Alfajumble, an obvious source for those elusive components as well as social interaction. In my experience, AROC is one of the best marque clubs in the UK. Pay the subscription and you can get involved as much as you want. There is also a club shop where all kinds of memorabilia and souvenirs – including, hopefully, this book – are available.

The British AROC magazine hasn't changed radically in the twelve years or so that I've been a club member, but Michael Lindsay has managed to rationalize production on a more regular bimonthly basis, together with a stop-press bulletin, as well as putting out a newsletter between issues. Both these publications carry adverts for members' cars and spare parts for sale, so anyone looking for a well cared for Spider or a restoration project could do no better than start their quest here.

The Club magazine also carries reports and results of the AROC Championship, a thoroughly entertaining and none too daunting race series in which members grapple with one another in Alfa Romeo tin-tops. As I have said already, Spiders have been conspicuous by their absence in these events, with one or two notable exceptions like the 2000 Spider of Ian Jacobs and Colin Burnes back in the mid-1980s. All participating cars are fully prepared to racing spec. with appropriate suspension mods, stripped-out interiors, full harness seat belts, fire extinguishers, roll cages and fuel-tank protection, as I found when I converted the GTV6 into a racer in the late-eighties. Although I confess to having been regularly somewhere down the back of the field (well someone has to be), it taught me that you could do a lot of things on the track that you ought not to do on the road. And you can sharpen up your road technique by implementing some of these tricks, like late braking or sliding around roundabouts. Boy racer? Well yes, I suppose so. But the other guys out there were completely crazy. Sitting on the grid before the start, I always

thought, 'What am I doing here with all these people who belong in an asylum?' Going into the first turn was a little like Hyde Park Corner in the rush hour – you took a deep breath and hoped not to trade too much paint with the cars swarming around you. Then everything settled down and you could concentrate on your race-craft and, in my case, avoiding the perils of being lapped by the Class A modified cars. But all too soon the ten-lap race is over. It is excellent fun, though, provided you don't bend it. In my case, I couldn't afford to because it would have been a very long walk home from Cadwell Park or Brands Hatch. Whereas most competitors trailered their racecars to and from the circuits, I drove

Ian Jacobs and Colin Burnes shared this 2000 Spider in the AROC/Chris Knott Insurance Championship series in the mid-1980s.

The AROC also holds Practice days and evenings for members at Snetterton, Castle Combe, Mallory Park and Goodwood, where this boat tail Spider is getting an airing. The dented front valance suggests that the owner was a little too enthusiastic.

mine, you see. I soon came to the conclusion that you can't effectively race a car which you have any pride in, because that makes you too inhibited to take risks or be sufficiently committed in a red mist battle to win a corner. The backing of a generous sponsor would cushion any disasters resulting from that situation, of course.

TYRE DOUBT

Alfa Romeo saw to it that the classic Spider kept pace with tyre evolutions, but one thing they don't need to be is over-tyred. Most Spiders from the 1960s and even the 1970s were quite happy running on 165 x 14

Cinturatos or their equivalent, even though the car's ultimate performance was more than the rubber could cope with. But once the spoilers started appearing, tyre sizes had to go up, just to match the aesthetics. The 1987 Quadrifoglio and 1989 'facelift' car that I drove in an extensive test session of Spiders around Lydden Hill circuit near Canterbury were both on 195/60 x 15 P7s. Even though they were rear-wheel drive, they behaved much more like modern cars as a result, going around corners as if they were on rails. There was still the reassuring on–off throttle control, but not so much of the driving on a knife-edge which you can experience in a Duetto.

All Alfas of this generation are prone to

169

Two Spiders ready for the off – a 1987 Quadrifoglio and a 1990 late-model 2.0-litre ex-Bell and Colvill.

bump-steer, but the wider tyres perhaps soak up undulations better than the skinny ones. They are best inflated a little way above the manufacturer's recommended pressures – I settled on 30psi front 32psi rear, although this may not be to everyone's taste. My preference would be for a compromise in size, which I found in a 1986 Spider, a 2.0-litre car lent to me recently by Bell and Colvill for a magazine feature, which ran on 185/70 x 14 Pirelli P6s. There was still much of the delightful edginess about the car, but combined with much of the surefootedness of sticky modern rubber. Every roundabout and hilly corner negotiated was a time of excitement, sensing when grip would give way to slide and the rear of the car would try to overtake the front. Tyre technology moves on at quite a pace, and the control tyre in the Alfa race series back in 1989–90 was the BF Goodrich Comp TA, which would slide nice and progressively. Tyre brands come and go according to product effectiveness and dictates of the marketplace, and, currently, Yokohamas appear to be the boots to have: putting them on my Alfa 75 some five years ago provided a revelation.

However, if you were set on uprating its undoubtedly fine handling, you might fit a set of Spax or Koni dampers with harder settings at the front and softer ones at the rear. I seem to end up lowering most of my road cars, and apart from the hassles of negotiating 'sleeping policemen' or visiting friends who live down unmade tracks, the result is always a quicker car around the twisty bits. I have taken this suspension- doctoring route several times with various Alfas, and as well as getting the tyres right, it's probably the single most significant improvement you can make to a standard car.

TRIM FIGURES

What of the Spider's interior finish and ergonomics? Well, most sports cars are prone to leaks, and the extent to which you ship water on board seems to depend on the hood fit and intensity of the downpour. My worst experience with the soft-top up was in a brand-new MGB-RV8 that I was road-

testing for *CarWeek*, when I was drenched within twenty minutes of the storm and the carpets were awash. Not only did the hood not fit but the screen leaked as well. Second worst was at the wheel of a new Morgan Plus Four, but you may well ask what I was doing driving a Morgan with the top up any-way. Maybe I've just been fortunate never to have found a Spider lacking in the umbrella department. However, hoods do get left off in the rain, by accident or misguided bravado, so the interiors are obviously more vulnerable than those of tin-tops. And since fitting the tonneau was always a bit of a chore – there was certainly a knack to getting it to stretch right over the cockpit – some owners probably never bothered with it. It goes without saying that you should check under

The classic Spider's soft-top was always a paragon of efficiency. It could be unfastened and folded back while the car was stationary at traffic lights, if need be.

carpets and soundproofing underlay if contemplating buying a classic Spider.

That said, since the 1967 Spider Veloce, Alfa Romeo has never skimped on interior trim for its soft-tops, and it is only the passage of time which makes the Duetto cockpit with its vinyl seats seem rather austere nowadays. There were touches of sophistication, such as the glove compartment courtesy light, illuminated whether the side lights were switched on or not. Among the Alfa's principal characteristics are the instrument binnacles housing the principal dials ahead of the driver. They were always a nice touch, although I found the Alfetta-style armrest-door pulls on the later 105-series Spiders somewhat obstructive. People have always gone on about the 'Italian Ape' driving position, using it as an excuse for a damning road test report, but long-term ownership of Alfas suggests that tall people simply evolve a compromise with their car. What is at stake is the relationship of seat squab and backrest to steering wheel and pedals. As far as I'm concerned, this involves the stretched arms and bent legs approach, although this is perhaps to overstate the matter unnecessarily. The dished steering wheels that replaced the Duetto's flatter profile black Bakelite wheel went some way to alleviating the problem.

LEFT HOOKERS

Buyers who are after a classic Spider will inevitably see pristine imports on their travels, which will almost invariably be left-hand drive. To readers in the States, and indeed most of the rest of the world, this may seem a pathetically parochial point, but in Great Britain, left-hand drive can be a bit of a problem, especially on crowded, fast A-roads where overtaking is

often tricky. In these circumstances, you can of course see further around right-hand bends from your left-hooker, but you're not so well placed to see the cyclist, horse or pedestrian on your side of a left-hander. In the city, though, it can be a positive advantage as you can see gaps down the inside of traffic jams that are not otherwise apparent.

My own experience of left-hookers teaches you to hang back from the vehicle in front. That is, until some clever-clogs overtakes you and slides into the space you've been leaving ahead of you. At any rate, Brits with left-hand-drive Spiders are well placed for European touring. And, of course, should you be really averse to driving your Spider from the left-hand seat, it is possible to get conversions done to right-hand drive. The pedals and steering gear would need to be sourced from a UK-spec car, and for fuller details on this, check Bell and Colvill's work in Chapter 4.

As for importing a Spider yourself, refer once more to Chapter 4 and the problems my featured Alfa shipper experienced, and remember that taxes, shipping costs, insurance, import duty and customs clearance could very nearly double the cost of the car's purchase price. But whatever the inherent problems and expense, importation of a car can be fun, especially if you drive it back from Italy or wherever, and there's nothing like a spot of aggravation – so long as it's not recurring – to bond you to a car. Despite the strong pound, though, you'd be unlikely to buy one much more cheaply abroad than back in the UK, but it just might be original.

THE OPPOSITION

Another aspect of the classic Alfa Spider that made it so remarkable was that it outlived all its soft-top contemporaries, bar one. As I've said, in the 1960s the Alfa buyer

The 105-series Alfa Spider's chief rival was the Fiat 124 Spider, which was also produced in the Pininfarina factory. While the Alfa model was never seriously campaigned as a competition machine, the Fiat was developed by Abarth into a world-class rally car. This is a works 124 Abarth, crewed by Verini/Russo, which came 19th in the 1973 RAC Rally.

might have considered the E-type Jaguar, Austin Healey 3000, Morgan Plus 8 – the only survivor – the Sunbeam Tiger, or any of the Triumphs, TR4, 5 or 6. All of these had a reputation for being rather more macho in character, or at least the drivers might like to have seen themselves in this light. The Elan was smaller, nimbler and therefore slightly faster than the Alfa, perhaps. I say 'perhaps', because I had an Elan S4SE in the mid-seventies, and I remember being able to keep up with a 2.0-litre Spider in a straight line, but not able to pass it. That blasted governor!

Other cars similar in size to the long-lived and relatively sophisticated Alfa Spider which you might have considered along the way are the Sunbeam Alpine, the Jensen Healey, the Triumph TR7, the Morgan 4/4 and Plus Four, the Lancia Beta Monte Carlo, and, of course, the MGB. The

Spridgets of this world were the first rung on the sports car ladder and too lowly for consideration, while the Fiat X1/9, or the Lotus and Caterham Sevens – survivors to this day – were too small and spartan to make a valid comparison, and therefore don't count here.

The Alfa Spider's natural competitor was its Torinese sister, the Fiat 124 Spider. Built, painted and trimmed on a parallel line in the Pininfarina factory, the 124 Spider was powered by the enduring Fiat twin-cam engine, which rose in size during its long production life from 1,438cc through 1,608cc to 1,592cc, and from 1,756cc to 1,995cc. The 124 Spider was made from 1966 to 1985, and over the years its styling underwent three evolutions, most notably to do with the adoption of federal bumpers. As with the Alfa Spider, they were also detrimental to the

Built on the Punto platform, the Fiat Barchetta was naturally smaller than the Tipo/155-derived Alfa Spider, but both cars were the product of Centro Stile, and both were launched in 1995.

purity of the bodywork. After production was handed over entirely to Pininfarina, the later 1983–5 models were equipped with Lancia's Volumex superchargers. A small number in the US got IHI turbochargers, which went some way to combating the performance-sapping emissions controls. Unlike the Alfa Spider, though, the Fiat 124 Spider had a serious competition pedigree, flaunted in its rally derivative, the Fiat Abarth 124 *Stradale* or CSA, which was homologated and developed for international rallying after Fiat bought out Abarth in 1971. The team scooped the European rally series honours in 1972, 1973 and 1975, by which time the cars sported exotic 16-valve heads and the

formidable driving talents of Hannu Mikkola and Marku Alen. Mikkola's navigator in 1975 was one Jean Todt.

The Fiat 124 Spider's creature comforts were somehow more grown-up than the Alfa's. Its hood was of better quality, and there were even rear quarter-light windows that rolled down inside the rear hood-well. It even qualified as a two-plus-two, as the space at the rear of the cockpit was scooped into a pair of child-size seats. It was never made in right-hand drive, however, and was thus something of a rarity in the UK.

Other than the Fiat 124 Spider, best value of the Alfa's competitors would probably have been the evergreen chrome-bumpered MGB, dated circa 1969. Basic and reliable, its overdrive gearbox and knotchy shift would go some way to matching the Spider's benchmark five. Although more spartan in appointment than the Alfa, the classic MGB had leather seats and a hood system equally as efficient as the Alfa's, although inferior in quality, and a B could cover long distances quite comfortably two and even three-up. I have done runs from the Paul Ricard circuit in France and the Österreichring in Austria back to Britain in just this fashion in an MGB. Perhaps that's why the car ended up with a dropped valve on one of these occasions, when it was just too overloaded to keep up with a Porsche 356B! The advantage an MGB has over a classic Alfa Spider is, of course, price, although they have long since calmed down from the heady days of 1988 when you could ask virtually what you liked for any classic car. Despite the fact that the B is hanging on as everyman's classic sports car, a good example can still be bought for around £3,000–£4,000, and you would be hard-pressed to find a really good Alfa Romeo for under £5,000. With the difference, you could endow your MGB with a stage two tuning kit and get the suspension worked over by someone like Ron Hopkinson, when its performance would be more than a match for that of a standard classic Spider. Its ride, however, wouldn't have been out of place in Jurassic Park. Nowadays, they're not particularly common, and a restored MGB with a British Heritage body shell could be as good as new.

The Barchetta cockpit was cosier than the Alfa's, and its dashboard and controls were much more innovative in concept.

If a final analysis were to be called for in the classic sports car stakes, I would always plump for the Alfa, because its styling in its purest form is more outstanding, more extrovert than the Fiat 124 Spider, although admittedly this too has its share of quirks. And the classic Alfa's handling offers more thrills and the ride is way better than the workaday MGB. Even in its most recent guise, it felt like a dinosaur. In a back-to-back test between a TVR Chimaera and an MGB RV8 when I was researching a book in 1993, I found the poor MG hopelessly outmoded as it pitched along country roads and searched for traction even on decent quality blacktop. Despair turned to annoyance as I reflected on the Rover Group's wasted opportunity.

But of course they had the MGF up their sleeve at the time.

But I digress. Back in 1983, Peter Nunn wrote in *Classic and Sportscar* magazine that 'lower running costs and a less exotic temperament' might tip the balance in the Fiat's direction, but the lack of expert help in the UK would help make the Alfa the winner. However, later on in 1990, when imported Fiats were more common in the UK, *Classic and Sportscar* ran an objective appraisal of this segment of the classic sports car market. They voted in favour of the Fiat 124 Spider as 'best buy', in preference to the Alfa Spider. But good as it is – and I have written a book about them – ultimately, the Fiat lacks the Alfa's charisma.

Who said it wasn't a family car? The Spider managed perfectly well on the school run and was a huge hit with the playground fraternity, as Alfie, Zoë and Bryony would confirm.

On a bumpy road, the Spider revealed that antediluvian phenomenon known as scuttle-shake. The multi-link rear suspension was firm enough to dislodge fillings if the car dipped into a pothole.

The modern Fiat Barchetta? Now there's another matter! This two-seater was styled in-house, and launched in 1995, almost on top of the new Alfa Spider – while, furthermore, both sportsters had coupé siblings, although Fiat's was quite radically different from its open-top sister. Like the Alfa, the Barchetta was rotund, but in a more traditional BMW Z3 or MX5 sort of way, rather than Elan fashion. Being based on the Punto platform rather than that of the larger Tipo, the Barchetta was naturally a much more compact package than the Alfa Spider. But its styling cues also included a slash along the side, and lighting arrangements that were in their own way quite as distinctive as the Alfa's. Its quirky flip-out door handles, reminiscent of the semaphore-arm indicators of the fifties, were an area of design neglected on the Spider but majored on in the new Alfa 156 saloon car, where they might just as easily have come from the doors of a Giulia Super. Apart from a clear gap in build quality, where the Barchetta and the Spider really parted company was in the area of their performance. The Fiat was powered by the four-cylinder 1,747cc 16-valve twin-cam, managing 130bhp and a competent, but far from phenomenal, 124mph (198kph) and 0-60mph (0-100kph) time of 8.9sec. The Barchetta's interior was more adventurous in design as well, with more swoops and curves about the dash, and a prominent trio of black-on-white instrument dials. It was perhaps a case of cuteness versus sophistication. Apart from that, the specification of the 'little boat' was not so dissimilar from the Spider's, providing ABS and all the latest safety features. And also, it promised to be rather more exclusive, and at £15K was a cool five grand cheaper than the new Alfa, in the UK at least. But do we mind if cars that are meant to be perceived as at least semi-exotic are in fact based on much more humble underpinnings like the Tipo and Punto? Presumably we should not, since the Duetto shared the Giulia Super platform and the Fiat 124 Spider was built on that of the even more prosaic 124 saloon. I reflected that if a Punto-based soft-top was eligible for consideration in this company, then what about the charming Bertone-styled Punto Cabriolet, combining rag-roof kicks with four-seater practicality?

DRIVING THE NEW SPIDER

Not that I'm a poseur or anything, but this new Spider is a great elevator of public esteem for the driver. Everyone loves the shape. During my tenure of the press car, neighbours spoke enviously – had I won the lottery? – schoolboys gasped in admiration, and people who'd previously ignored me now found themselves able to communicate. (But when the car went back, would they still be speaking?)

I loved the shape too. But would the driving of it measure up? Initial impressions were promising, although there was dissent in the ranks over the interior. You don't have to be a vegan to object to leather upholstery. You either like it or loathe it, and my wife Laura felt nauseated by the smell of it in our test car. So I guess we would have to strike that off the options list. But being new, the seats were firmer and more supportive than most of the classic models I have driven, which was a plus point. My daughter Zoë thought the upholstery of the press car should have been red as well as the exterior, and there was a time thirty or forty years ago when manufacturers offered such hues as a matter of course. You could certainly specify late-model classic Spiders with light tan leather, and of course in a bespoke car like the Morgan you can have more or less whatever colour trim you like.

Test cars have always extended into a family affair here, and the children's opinions are often valid. They insisted on being taken to and from school in the Spider and their playground credibility was enhanced enormously. Normally I buckled both of them into the passenger seat while the dog posed on the parcel shelf behind. (Even back in 1969, John Bolster wrote in *Autosport* that this space in a Spider was 'ideal for dogs'.) It's interesting to reflect that before the era of seat belts, we thought nothing of undertaking long journeys in sports cars, with passengers perched on the transmission tunnel or crouched on the shelf behind the seats. Now though, there was a big question-mark over the legality of carrying children, not to mention the safety aspect of so doing. However, on a weekend run with both children in the back of the Spider, we passed in full view of a police 'jam sandwich' and they offered not the slightest hint of concern. So that must be all right then.

There was nothing to complain about with the Spider's controls. Everything felt precise and modern. One turn on the key and the engine fired up from cold, the automatic choke sustaining its running. The

The current Spider is gorgeous to look at, well mannered, reliable and competent – provided the road surface is smooth – when it has that safe and secure 'cornering on rails' composure.

gear lever's knob is shaped a bit like a walking stick handle, so your fingers cup it nicely. The gear change itself is average by modern standards, but it is not the positive experience of the old Spider's shift. There were a few minor rattles from the dashboard and around the glove locker, and creaks from the soft-top. They were by no means intrusive, and only evident if you listened out for them. Maybe the stiffer coupé body of the GTV doesn't suffer from them, but the main thing was that the Spider inspired a feeling of strength and rigidity.

One of its strong points is its steering. Alfa's latest high-ratio rack-and-pinion steering – 2.2 turns lock-to-lock – is hydraulically power assisted and speed sensitive to provide precise and progressive steering. It certainly felt delicate, and was nicely balanced for town driving. It was claimed to be the most direct of any car in current production. You have to be extremely sensitive to make judgments as fine as that, but it was true that manoeuvrability on crowded city streets and agility in tight traffic situations were superb, and spontaneous changes of lane or road positioning could be accomplished with complete confidence. Straight line stability on main roads was excellent too, with a well-weighted degree of self-centring.

The new Spider's suspension was a good deal firmer than I'd anticipated, especially the rear, which was of a softer set up on the classic Spiders. The result was that 'sleeping policemen' and other so-called traffic-calming measures produced a loud bonk from the back end. And, more significantly, you could feel every bump along the notoriously poorly surfaced roads of north Norfolk, undulations that the classic Spiders as well as the Alfa 75 just soaked up in their stride. This begs the question as to why Alfa designed the new car's suspension to be compliant just on billiard-table flat

surfaces, when there are some truly shocking roads not far from where the cars are actually built.

It didn't bottom out on a notorious switch-back section I regularly travel on, however, a place where the 75 flattens its downpipes at anything like the ton, and I have resorted to backing off now, in order to ease the load on the cheque book if not the stomach-in-mouth effect. So clearly there's something to be said for a harder rear set-up. But it's not just the back end that registers every bump with a thump. The phenomenon is fed back through the steering wheel, and if the car dipped into anything approaching a pothole, it was accompanied by rather unpleasant vibrations that I could only assume to be scuttle shake. This surprised me, but presumed that being an open car, the Spider must still suffer from this antediluvian shortcoming. It seemed far worse than I had experienced with the classic cars, but perhaps being a new model, my expectations were rather higher. I swapped notes later with a senior member of the Alfa Romeo Owners' Club – who declined to be quoted on this matter – and he said he'd had a similar experience to mine, driving the new GTV over bumpy roads, although without the Spider's scuttle shake.

On new-laid tarmac its ride was wonderful, although there is a tendency for it to pitch, to dip and dive, making it turn into corners relatively sharply. I'd say that the power steering is a tad too sensitive, but you get used to things like this, especially if you're used to front-wheel drive. Initially at least I found I was driving the Spider with the steering wheel rather than using the accelerator pedal to control oversteer. This was surprising, since front-drive cars respond to nothing more than throttle variations to bring the nose in or out. Instead, I found I was turning the wheel to change direction, to adjust the line in mid-corner.

One wonders to what extent the multi-link rear end affects the handling of the car. Apart from the excellent turn-in – on smooth blacktop, anyway – you are not really aware of the rear-wheel steering aspect of the multi-link set-up. To understand the philosophy behind it, and how it works in practice, you need to appreciate what happens when you steer a car into a corner. In a left-hander, as the front wheels turn in, the tyres generate a lateral force that pushes the nose of the car to the left and tries to spin the entire car about its centre of gravity. Clearly, if the rear tyres had no grip, this would make the tail of the car swing outwards to the right. Instead, the grip exerted by the rear tyres tends to compress the suspension arms between the wheels and the car. However, in the Spider's multi-link system, compression only occurs in the elastic bushes lining each of the joints, so the hub of the right rear wheel, for example, moves fractionally to the left. But no such compression takes place in the joints of the steering link, because they are designed to resist it, and since the link is ahead of the hub, it steers the right wheel slightly to the right. The effect of this is to accentuate what the front wheels are doing, encouraging the whole car to change direction. In practice, it gives the steering a feeling of greater alacrity and more acute turn-in.

However, if this condition was allowed to carry on, it would result in the undesirable effect of the rear tyres allowing the tail to drift outwards, which would reduce the overall cornering power of the car. It does not last more than a fraction of a second, because as the car rolls, the outer wheel is forced upwards, relative to the Spider body shell. The pivoting suspension arms continue to control the right rear wheel in the vertical plane, but the 'steering' link describes its own subtly different arc,

pulling the front of the hub carrier inwards and thus steering the wheel to the left, in accord with the front wheels. We are only talking about a very slight movement, but it ensures that the rear tyres generate their maximum cornering power while maintaining the stability of the steering. It makes the front-drive car go where it's pointed without any rear-end waywardness. It tacks unerringly through high-speed corners, provided the surface is even.

In practical terms, the difference between front-wheel drive and the rear-wheel drive cars is that the former feels in its way much more stable, particularly through high-speed corners. But there's nothing like the degree of feedback that you get from a rear-drive car. It's certainly not alive in the same way that the classic Spider is. Obviously the response you do get, relative to the power delivery, is through the front wheels rather than the back. The Spider's ABS brakes are impressive indeed, and extremely effective, providing tremendous stopping power in any situation, and putting those of its predecessors in the shade. I did experience a curious lack of feel under heavy braking though.

The accompanying soundtrack of the rasping Twin Spark motor is pleasant enough, and while not as inspiring as the blood-curdling howl of the V6, it is quite as sonorous under throttle as the old twin-cam. Smoother, in fact. It rises from a dull, muffled hum at a low 2,000rpm, but when you climb up through the revs you get the characteristic throaty gargle. It just lopes along at a modest 3,500rpm at the legal speed limit.

In performance terms, there's no denying the latest Twin Spark engine is a gem. Perhaps not quite the pearl its predecessor was (I had an ex-Alfa GB 75 TwinSpark for a while) but it does love to rev, and it is responsive right the way through the

1. The plastic hood cover is raised so that the rear of the hood can be lifted out of its recess.

range, providing ample torque to pull smartly away at low revs as well. I think it seems stronger than the old Twin Spark. More relevant to the character of the car is that it feels like it really wants to get up and go at about 90mph (145kph). It has the similar sort of acceleration as my 3.0-litre 75, but you have to drop a couple of cogs to get the same effect. This is nowhere more important than when climbing up a long hill, where it really does run out of breath if you don't change down. It also pays to drop a cog to get the best out of a fast bend.

Happily, one thing that you don't suffer from is torque steer under acceleration, which was the bane of most powerful front-drive cars, including the 164. The Spider felt at its most stable between 100- and 120mph (160–193kph), but curiously, it didn't seem to want to go much more than that. Perhaps the test car's engine had yet to loosen up sufficiently. In some ways the more I drove this car the more sense it made, and the faster I went the better it seemed.

All devotees of rear-wheel drive must think twice before committing themselves

2. *The hood is unclipped at the windscreen header rail and lifted back.*

3. *The frame's hinges allow the canopy to fold down almost of its own accord.*

4. *With a bit of help, the folded hood is pushed down into its recess, after which the plastic cover is pressed home on either side of the car.*

5. *To erect the hood, the process is simply reversed. The plastic cover is released with a button inside the right-hand doorjamb.*

to owning, or even praising, a front-drive car. Why has Alfa become so committed to it, you wonder, when BMW among others can still produce rear-drive vehicles? It has to be a cost-saving measure, because it is to the manufacturer's advantage that the whole drivetrain can be pre-assembled with a degree of shared parts-bin componentry, and it is ready to be slotted in place into the shared platform. And in the Spider's case there is no propshaft or rear differential to bother with. They must have got their sums right, I suppose, because objectively, there is no doubt that the modern Spider can be driven very fast with absolute confidence.

GET YOUR TOP OFF

The raising of the hood (soft-top) involves the following sequence of operations. Firstly, you press the button in the hood recess that releases the mechanism for the hood cover. As this pops up, you can extricate the front hoop of the hood, bringing it up and out of its well. The hood's rear hoop is also lifted out of the well. Then the plastic hood cover is closed, needing firm pressure on either side. Using a similar amount of pressure, you lock the rear hoop into place. After stretching the hood right to the windscreen top rail, you then get inside the car and pull the hood's front hoop firmly home by the central finger-grip. And finally, it is fastened in position onto the windscreen header rail with J-shaped hooks that you operate by two handles hidden at either side of the hoop itself. The corners inside the rear three-quarter section of the hood are neatened up by pressing home a couple of Velcro strips behind the rear edges of the side window apertures.

You simply lower the hood by repeating each of the above operations in reverse

order, taking care to remember to close the front-hoop levers before shutting the hood cover. The practicality of the system is impressive, and it soon becomes an easy task to perform. I worry though about the long-term robustness of the plastic hood cover and the electric mechanism. Once or twice it seemed unwilling to respond, although I concede it may just be a matter of acclimatization. As a safety device, the hood cover will not open if the ignition key is not in the engine-off position.

Visibility is not bad with the top up, although at first there is a hint of claustrophobia brought on by the shallow screen and side windows, and the surrounding blackness of hood interior and leather upholstery. You soon become acclimatized to this though. The back window plastic already had a slight crease across the centre, which at this early stage in the car's life did not bode well. That's obviously why you can easily zip in a new window. However, for a while, I was conscious of the creased plastic when viewing the traffic behind in the rear mirror.

Reversing into tight spaces proved strangely problematic, taking on proportions of an inordinately perplexing nature, and once or twice I cursed my own ineptitude. Not only did the car's rounded shoulders pose a visibility problem with regard to kerbs and other vehicles, but the rear three-quarter visibility with the hood erect also made life more difficult. You couldn't easily judge where the back rear corners of the car were. But there was more. I think it may have been to do with the power steering, which was perhaps too compliant in a parking situation, not allowing the driver to feel precisely what the tyres were actually up to.

Driving in rain with the top up and a full complement of passengers on board, the back window tended to mist up, but a blast with the fan put that to rights. Wind noise around 80mph (125kph) was quite marked, although as with any sports car, you expect conversation to be a battle. When we tried out the radio-cassette player, turning down the Tamla was only a problem when we slowed in a built-up area. Most importantly, however, the top showed absolutely no sign of leaking during a heavy downpour, while the wipers did their job properly.

However, the wipers' delay mechanism did prove to be the most enigmatic of all the Spider's gadgetry. It operates by means of a twist-grip on the end of the stalk on the right of the steering column, and the wipers make a stab at moving but they can't as there's something restraining them. And then they go. And then they sit still for a bit, parked halfway across the screen. Then they go again. It turns out to be a variable speed adjustment, and the further around you twist it, the more frequently it sweeps the windscreen. All very well, but the tendency to park mid-screen on intermittent function was a trifle frustrating.

The boot (trunk) can be unlocked internally by a button inside the glove compartment, or externally with the key, by swivelling the Alfa badge to one side to reveal the lock. Boot space has never been a factor to bother sports car devotees, although the classic Spider could probably accommodate more than the new car. The spaces are shaped differently. One's boot is

Wind-in-the-hair motoring may be a bit of a cliché, but the passenger in this 1969 1750 Spider Veloce seems to be getting into it. For a more entertaining drive, the vivacious oldster could be the one to go for.

flat and shallow, while the other's is narrow and deep. Where the former slots its spare wheel away in a sunken well, the latter's none-too-compact space-saver occupies potential storage space. The new Spider's battery is hidden under the parcel shelf – the dog's seat – within the cockpit. The bonnet is raised by pulling the lever under the steering column, lifting the safety catch to the right of the grille, and raising it with the assistance of two gas struts.

What has happened to the Pininfarina logo, I wondered? As on the current Fiat Coupé, its presence on the Spider is barely discernible now, and it is certainly a shadow of the distinctive 'f' badge which appeared on the flanks of the classic Spiders – Fiat as well as Alfa Romeo.

What about the competition for the new Spider? Well, to be in with a shout they have to be good looking. There are dearer cars on the market, like the TVR Griffith (£34K), Mercedes-Benz SLK (£30K), BMW Z3 (£21–28K), and Porsche Boxter (£34K). More austere for around the same money (at 1998 prices) are the Caterham Seven and 21 (£21–25K), the Morgan 4/4 (£20K), the Lotus Elise (£20K), and of course the second-generation Lotus Elan, which was actually not austere at all. This model is still available, having resurfaced in the Far East as a Kia Sport in 1995 after its short life as a Lotus, the Hethel firm having sold off the moulds and tooling to the Koreans.

It was not only its round-edged low-nose, high-tail shape that made the Elan/Kia a natural comparison with the Alfa Spider. The SE (special equipment) version was powered by the 1.6-litre Isuzu-Lotus turbocharged 16-valve transverse four, and as it produced 165bhp at 6,600rpm, it was actually somewhat quicker than the Spider, as well as being a bit more nimble. Subtract the IHI turbo, and you were left with the 130bhp normally aspirated base model,

which was proportionally less rapid. As a Kia Sport, the car is now powered by a 151bhp 1.8-litre twin-cam unit, and is seen by the Korean company as an MGF rival, priced at around £18K. It thus undercuts its progenitor by some way, since the Elan was priced at £20K at its launch in 1990, but whether it will tempt potential Spider buyers in its latest incarnation is a moot point. When the Elan SE was new, the main gripe was that the single-layer soft-top was below par, and although performance and handling were of the highest order, it was just not an interesting car to drive, which, if nothing else, was what you'd expect a Lotus to be.

And that, in a way, sums up how I feel about the Spiders, really. The current car, while gorgeous to look at, well mannered, reliable and very competent, given that pristine road surface, is just not anywhere near as much fun or as interesting to drive as the classic Spider. They both turn heads, so image is not a problem whichever one you are driving. Clearly, at half the cost of a new model, your bank balance is likely to favour the acquisition of one of the classic Spiders. But in the final analysis, I have to say that if it's an entertaining drive you're after, the vivacious oldster with its rear-wheel drive is the one to go for.

But hold on a minute. Aren't we forgetting something? They fit the Spider and the GTV with the glorious 24-valve 3.0-litre V6 engine, don't they? It's just that they don't import them into the UK, at least not yet. Surely that gutsy six-pot motor has got to swing the balance the other way? Having sat behind one of these engines (12-valves only) for 100,000 miles or so, I can testify that its 192bhp, not to mention its aural delights, make a very strong case for another trip to Bell and Colvill. Or for hanging on until Alfa GB starts importing the 3.0-litre Spider into the UK.

Appendix

Useful Addresses

Some useful addresses and phone numbers for Spider owners and buyers in the UK (accurate at March 1998):

1900 Register
Peter Marshall
Mariners
Courtlands Avenue
Esher, Surrey

2600 Register
Roger Monk
Knighton
West Runton
Cromer, Norfolk

Alfarama
Westmoreland Road
London NW9 9RL
0171-206 2075

Alfa Romeo Giulia 105 Register
Chris Sweetapple
The Highwood Motor Company
(Alfa Romeo replacement panels,
workshop manuals on CD-ROM)
137 Bishopston Road
Swansea SA3 3EX

Alfa Romeo Giulietta Register
Peter Shaw
Grange Farm House
2 Bedford Road
Willington
Bedfordshire MK44 3PS

Alfa Romeo Owners' Club
Secretary: Michael Lindsay
97 High Street
Linton
Cambridge CB1 6JT
01223 894300

Alfa Romeo Owners' Club Shop
Ray Skilling
EM Models
42 Camden Road
Tunbridge Wells
Kent TN1 2QD
01892 536689

Alfa II
(Alfa servicing, sales)
Unit 5
Parr Road
Stanmore HA7 1NL
0181 951 4100

Alfa Stop
(Classic Alfa brake and exhaust
 systems specialists)
PO box 50
Belper
Derbyshire DE56 1AS
0177 382 2000

Automeo
(Alfa Romeo servicing, spares, maintenance; carburettor specialist)
Les Dufty
36 Gypsy Patch Lane

Little Stoke
Bristol
0117 969 5771

Richard Banks
(Classic Alfa Romeo and Italian car
 sales)
Oakford, Tiverton
Devon
01398 351360

Bell and Colvill
(Alfa Romeo Spider specialists)
Bobby Bell or Martin Colvill
Epsom Road
West Horsley
Surrey KT24 6DG
014865 4671

Benalfa Cars
(Alfa Romeo restorations, engine
 rebuilds)
Alan Bennett
19 Washington Road
West Wilts Trading Estate
Westbury
Wiltshire
01373 864333

Brookside Garage
(Classic Alfa Romeo specialists,
 competition preparation)
Jon Dooley
55 High Street
Wrestlingworth
Sandy, Beds
01767 23217

T.A. & J.M. Coburn
(Alfa Romeo soft-top and
 upholstery specialists)
Widhill House
Blunsdon
Swindon, Wilts
01793 721501

Richard Drake Motors
(Alfa Romeo servicing, engine rebuilds,
 race preparation)
Unit 2, Renson Close
Beech Drive
Mile Cross Lane
Norwich NR6 6RH
01603 406050

**EB Spares (The Italian
 Connection)**
David Edgington
31 Link Road
Westbury Trading Estate
Westbury
Wilts BA13 4JB
01373 823856

Gran Turismo Engineering
(Classic Alfa Romeo specialists, sales,
 race preparation)
Simon Whiting
Station Avenue
Kew Gardens, Surrey
0171 460 0007

Italian Miniatures
(Alfa Romeo models)
Richard Crompton
39 Penncricket Lane
Oldbury, Warley
West Midlands B68 8LX
0121 559 6611

K & L Autos
Keith Waite
(Mobile servicing of classic Alfas)
Golders Green, London N5
0181 458 3879 or 0585 655503

Lombarda Carriage Company
(Alfa spares and sales)
3–10 Railway Mews
London W10 6HN
0171 243 0638

MGS Coachworks
(Alfa restoration specialists)
Mike Spenceley
Foxley Hill Road
Purley
Surrey CR8 2HB
0181 645 0555

Richard Norris
(Classic Alfa Romeo spares specialist)
44A The Gardens
East Dulwich
London SE22 9QQ
0181 299 2929

Jamie Porter
(Alfa servicing, spares,
   rolling road, maintenance)
Rowland House
Lower Gower Road
Royston, Herts
01920 822987

Ramponi Rockell
(Alfa Romeo sales)
30–31 Lancaster Mews
London W2 3QE
0171-262 7383

Rossi Engineering
Rob Giordanelli
(Race preparation, restoration,
   maintenance)
Sunbury on Thames, Surrey
01932 786819

Jonathan Smith
Carsmiths
(105-series restorations, maintenance,
   replica GTAs built)
Ashwellthorpe Industrial Estate
Wymondham, Norfolk
01508 489508

Spider's Web
(Secondhand spares for
   classic Alfa spares)
Roger Longmate
Swaffham, Norfolk
01760 756229

Touring Superleggera
Andrew Thorogood
(Classic Alfa restoration,
   race preparation)
Putney, London SW15
0181 780 3455 or 0589 433461

Julius Thurgood
(Classic Alfa sales, competition
   car specialist)
Broomfield Farm
Coleshill Road
Bentley
Warwicks CV9 2JS
01827 720361

Timeless Motor Company
(Overhauls, repairs, restorations)
John Timpany
Poole's Lane
Highwood
Chelmsford
Essex
01245 248008

Veloce Cars
(Secondhand Alfa sales, spares)
Romford, Essex
0181 551 0644

Zagato Register
Franco Macri
Kenfield Hall
Petham, Canterbury
Kent CT4 5RN

Index

Index